Praise for
ROWING THE NORTHWEST PASSAGE

"Climate change is happening so rapidly in the Arctic that it is absolutely essential that people go there and intelligently record what they see, as Kevin Vallely so compellingly does in *Rowing the Northwest Passage*."

PETER WADHAMS, author of *A Farewell to Ice*

"A thrilling adventure tale in which each hard mile not only reveals the strength of the human spirit but also hammers home the hard truths of climate change."

CAMERON DUECK, author of *The New Northwest Passage*

"A compelling page-turner of an adventure story."

ROZ SAVAGE, Guinness World Record-setting ocean rower

"Vallely transports the reader to places few will ever go: the very edges of the earth and of human endurance."

EVAN SOLOMON, host of CTV's *Question Period*

"A must-read for any Arctic or Northwest Passage enthusiast or for anyone concerned about our planet's future in the face of global warming."

CAPTAIN KENNETH K. BURTON,
Executive Director, Vancouver Maritime Museum

"Combines a fantastic tale of adventure with an important message on the state of our environment. Vallely's writing keeps the reader engaged with beautiful descriptions of the people, landscapes and wildlife he encounters."

COLIN ANGUS, author & *National Geographic* Adventurer of the Year

"What this modern saga of the Northwest Passage brings to light is the new image of the passage as canary in the coal mine. A warning sign of vast planetary changes—caused by us —and threatening our future."

ELIZABETH MAY, leader of the
Green Party of Canada and MP for Saanich—Gulf Islands

"A powerful call to action wrapped in a rich tale of adventure, history and the harsh reality of a changing climate."

ERIC SOLOMON, Director, Arctic Connections at the Vancouver Aquarium

LLELY

ROWING
THE
NORTHWEST
PASSAGE

ADVENTURE, FEAR, AND AWE
IN A RISING SEA

GREYSTONE BOOKS
Vancouver/Berkeley

To my Dad whose spirit is with me always and to my Mom
whose unwavering support has never faltered.

Greystone Books Ltd.
www.greystonebooks.com

Cataloguing data available from Library and Archives Canada
ISBN 978-1-77164-134-0 (pbk.)
ISBN 978-1-77164-135-7 (epub)

Editing by Lynne Melcombe
Copy editing by Stephanie Fysh
Cover and text design by Naomi MacDougall
Cover photograph by Kevin Vallely
Photographs by Denis Barnett,
Kevin Vallely, and Frank Wolf
Printed and bound in Canada on
ancient-forest-friendly paper by Friesens

We gratefully acknowledge the support of the Canada Council for the Arts, the British Columbia Arts Council, the Province of British Columbia through the Book Publishing Tax Credit, and the Government of Canada for our publishing activities.

CONTENTS

INTRODUCTION

I SOWED THE FIRST SEEDS of an idea to traverse the Northwest Passage two decades ago during a conversation with friend and world-class adventurer Jerome Truran. It was a casual chat about what adventuring world firsts remained to be done. We agreed that traversing the Northwest Passage under human power in a single season was at the top of the list. But at the time, it was impossible. The Northwest Passage didn't open up for long enough during the summer months to contemplate such a feat. Our idea remained just that.

I was an active outdoor athlete taking part in an array of adventure sports, from rock climbing to kayaking, backcountry skiing to trail running, but I had never undertaken an expedition. I was enamored of the idea of striking out and doing something unique, testing my limits in the spirit of true adventure. I had no idea those early yearnings would chart a life course that would steer me toward a career in exploration.

The Arctic has interested me since I was a child. My father operated a radio at the Hopedale Mid-Canada Line station on the northern Labrador coast in the early 1960s, and his stories of his time there fascinated me. He was a new immigrant to Canada from Limerick, Ireland, and this was his first job in his new country. Isolated and remote, Hopedale was one of a series of radar stations that ran across the middle of Canada to provide early warning of a Soviet bombing attack on North America. For a young man more accustomed to the temperate climate of southern Ireland, this wild new land couldn't have come as more of a shock. He told me of endless winter darkness and cold so intense, human skin would freeze in seconds. But he also talked of the ephemeral play of the aurora borealis as it danced across the inky night sky and of an exquisite silence broken only by the beating of his own heart. It was a world both terrifying and raw that could still seduce through wonder and surprise.

My father was one of only three working at Hopedale. One winter night just after a temporary construction crew had flown out from the facility, a fire broke out and the radar station burned to the ground. My father and the two other operators barely escaped with their lives and had to survive in a storage shed until rescuers could fly in. This, to me, was the epitome of excitement and adventure. I've seen the Arctic as a romantic landscape for as long as I can remember.

My first major expedition was in February 2000, when I skied the length of Alaska's 1,000-mile Iditarod Trail from Anchorage to Nome with two teammates. The journey opened my eyes to real adventure and I never looked back. In the coming years, I climbed active volcanoes in Java, Indonesia, in the midst of jihad, repeated a 1,250-mile Klondike-era ice-bike journey through the dead of an Alaskan winter, and became the first person since World War II to retrace the infamous Sandakan Death March through the jungles of Borneo.

A key adventure for me took place in 2007, when I traveled to the Canadian High Arctic to explore the beaches of King William Island, searching for clues from the doomed Franklin expedition. With the help of Inuit historian Louie Kamookak, I saw skeletal remains, likely from the Franklin crew, that were still scattered about the land and yet remained uninvestigated and untested. Evan Solomon, an anchorman for CBC Sunday-night news at the time and my teammate on the expedition, made a compelling documentary of our journey and discussed the political indifference being shown to a pivotal historical event in Canadian history. That was when I realized that an expedition could be more than a personal test of stamina; it could also be a vehicle for sharing an important message.

An adventure in 2009 drove that point home. That year, Ray Zahab, Richard Weber, and I broke the world record for the fastest unsupported trek from the edge of the Antarctic continent to the geographic South Pole. Throughout our journey, we maintained real-time communication with over 10,000 schoolchildren around the world. By the end of the journey, we'd garnered a staggering 1.5 billion media impressions. For me, this demonstrated the formidable reach a well-publicized expedition can garner when there's a worthwhile message to share.

By that time, my interest in climate change had been taking shape for a couple of years. It began in late 2006, after I watched Al Gore's documentary *An Inconvenient Truth,* which laid bare the scientific reality of global warming and made a powerful argument that the international community needed to do something quickly to avert a climate disaster. The following year, after returning from my expedition on King William Island, I learned that sea ice in the Arctic had declined to an unprecedented level over that summer—a full 23 percent less than the previous benchmark, set in 2005. This record was shattered again in 2012, when a further 300,000 square miles beyond the 2007 record melted. No models had predicted such a decline. Climate scientists were in shock.

That was when the seed of that idea planted in 1997 began to grow. The Northwest Passage had by then melted so much that it remained open for long stretches of time in the summer months, making a transit possible. If someone could make it across the Northwest Passage in a single season solely under human power, a preposterous notion just a few years earlier, the adventure would capture world attention and convey an irrefutable message. What better way to make a statement about climate change than to do something that was only possible because of climate change?

Everything else grew from there: assembling a team, commissioning a boat, getting a sponsor on board, and, of course, the trip itself. In some ways, the organization was routine. After all, by the time we embarked on this expedition, I was hardly a novice adventurer; this was my twelfth expedition. But the expedition itself was far from routine, and not only because of the adversity we encountered as adventurers. It was exceptional for all of us because we attempted to do something that had never even been done before, a significant opportunity for an adventurer. And although it sounds cliché, in some ways it was life-changing for me because I moved past the notion of undertaking an adventure purely for self-fulfillment to using it for a much larger purpose: to promote and encourage positive change in the world we all share. This realization made the journey both humbling and inspiring in ways that none of my previous expeditions had been.

I can't say that one of the things my time in the Arctic changed for me was my own opinions, because my opinions on climate change were well set before I headed off. But what did change was my sense of urgency. I wish there were some way I could provide everyone with an opportunity to enjoy the sort of up close and personal glimpse I had of the Arctic and its inhabitants, because then I'd have no doubt that everyone would share that sense of urgency. Of course, doing so would be impossible, but what I knew from the beginning was *not* impossible was to write and take pictures and hope that through my words and my eyes, others would feel enough of the experience vicariously to appreciate that urgency the way I do.

The Arctic is in the midst of profound change, but what's happening there is only a harbinger of what's to come for the rest of the planet. Humankind is at a crossroads. If we turn one way, it will be hard road but our future as a species will be assured. If we turn another way, we're gambling with the future of the planet. I fervently hope my voice in this book will help you decide to add *your* voice to the chorus calling for dramatic measures to avert a climate crisis now.

1

A LAST FIRST

THE TORTURED FORM OF A decaying piece of ice glides past us and disappears again into the fog, a weary foot soldier returning home from some distant battle. The hair-raising action of the last couple days has frayed our nerves, and rowing our boat blindly around the Arctic headland of Cape Parry between large chunks of ice isn't helping. The wind died at two-thirty this morning when a cold, stagnant Arctic air mass took its place and we jumped at our opportunity to move. This is the first calm weather we've experienced in days, and we treat it as a change in our fortunes. We couldn't be more wrong.

It's July 31, 2013, as Frank Wolf and I are rowing our four-person ocean rowing boat, the *Arctic Joule,* through the waters of the Amundsen Gulf on the Northwest Passage. Our teammates, Paul Gleeson and Denis Barnett, are resting in the stern cabin awaiting their turn on the oars. The visibility is a mere fifty yards, but we're forced to travel solely by the aid of GPS and compass. We know we're close to the cape from the steady thump of waves against cliff, but we see nothing.

The seas change as we round Cape Parry, with house-sized rollers, dark and foreboding, rising out of nowhere, sweeping beneath our hull and disappearing again into the murk. The rhythm of the swell is like the deep breathing of some oceanic giant rousing from its slumber, the crash of wave on rock its wake-up call.

We rise and fall with the pulse of the ocean, but we're blind in this world of white. The steady rumble of surf to starboard helps us navigate, and the sound of breaking waves feels ominous. It's not long before the echoes from the cape begin to surround us—one moment to starboard, then to port, then back to starboard again—and we become completely disoriented. "We need to get away from these cliffs," I yell to Frank. "It's too dangerous this close to the cape." The sound of breaking waves envelops us. "We're spinning in circles," Frank says after checking the GPS. "We're caught in a current or something."

We try everything to right ourselves, but it's hopeless; our boat is gripped by an invisible force and we can't regain control. In the confusion we fail to notice the building wind until it explodes upon us, driving us straight out to sea. Just offshore, about six miles away, sits the pack ice, and we're now headed straight for it. If we reach it, we'll be crushed.

I clamber into the cabin and check the navigation screen of our onboard GPS. I wonder if we have space to outrun the pack ice if we fight the wind and head south. The pack ice is big, the winds are intensifying, and we don't have control of the boat. "Not likely," I mumble. As I stare blankly at the navigation screen, I see it. I hadn't noticed it earlier on the handheld

GPS, but there appears to be an island between us and the pack. Called Bear Island, it's a mere speck, maybe a hundred yards wide, but if we can make it there, we might save ourselves. It's our only chance.

We hold a straight line going southeast, 45 degrees to the wind-driven waves, and start rowing for all we're worth. The seas continue to build and the fog remains thick. The waves are hitting us hard to starboard as we battle cross seas to a point several miles upwind from the island and make our turn. The scream of the wind dies immediately and we start to glide with it. "It's like landing a paraglider on a postage stamp," Frank says, the only words we've shared in the last thirty minutes. Surfing among the white-capped rollers, we race toward our invisible island in the fog.

When we're within a mile or two, I scream to Paul and Denis to get out on deck. "Put on your dry suits, guys!" They scramble out of the cabin, fully aware of what's been unfolding. "Tell us when you see the island," I shout. It becomes obvious now that facing backward in a rowboat can be very impractical at times.

"We're four hundred meters out," Frank yells (about four hundred yards). "Do you see anything?"

"Nothing," Paul replies.

A moment later, Frank yells, "Two hundred meters out."

"Nothing," Paul says. "Wait a moment, I think I see—"

We all hear it before we see it—the deep, resonating thud of wave against cliff. I strain my neck over my left shoulder to see Bear Island ringed in steep cliffs, huge waves, and little hope. Our island refuge is no salvation at all.

We begin to traverse around the island to see if there's any potential landing point. "Over there!" Paul screams. He's pointing to a steep rocky beach, maybe forty yards wide. "Can we land on that?" It's totally exposed to the waves, but it's our only choice.

We're pushed in hard. Paul steers as Frank and I maintain a steady row. As we hit the beach, in a drill we mastered on Sellwood Bay earlier in this trip, Paul and Denis leap out and keep the stern perpendicular to the surf.

"I'm going to see if there's a better landing spot," I yell as I jump out of the boat. I sprint up the rocky shore and nearly fall flat on my face, my sea legs getting the better of me.

Bear Island is tiny and takes only a couple of minutes to survey. "This is it, guys!" I shout out as I return to the boat. "It's cliff the entire way around this thing."

Denis and I begin to set up a winch-pulley system while Frank and Paul control the boat. We lasso several enormous slabs of rock as an anchor for the winch, but they shift under load when we start hauling the *Arctic Joule* ashore. We push a smooth-faced driftwood log beneath the hull in hopes it will help the boat roll, but the raging surf keeps pushing the stern up and sideways, tossing the log out from below. The beach is simply too steep and the boat too heavy for us to haul it completely out of the water.

Our winch system is acting as our anchor, and we fear that if the rope snaps, the *Arctic Joule* will be set adrift in the maelstrom. We pull two large duffel bags out from the bow of the boat, position them on opposite sides of the winch anchor, and fill them with rocks. We tie lines between the rock-laden bags and the boat, hoping that their weight will take some of the strain off the winch and act as a backup if it fails. It's a tenuous solution, but it's all we have.

I'm not sure how we could have avoided this predicament. A ground anchor, if we still had one, wouldn't have helped us coming around the cape; the water was too deep. A robust sea anchor could have helped, but the one we have isn't capable of holding us in one place. We built our equipment kit based on information garnered from rowing teams that had made successful open ocean traverses, but we're discovering now how different that is from a traverse of the Northwest Passage. Deploying a sea anchor in the middle of the Atlantic Ocean and getting blown off course by ten miles is one thing. Deploying a sea anchor in the Northwest Passage and getting blown onto cliffs or into grinding pack ice is another matter entirely. Somehow we managed to hit this tiny islet in the midst of a storm with zero visibility. Had we missed it, we would have been pushed straight out into the grinding pack ice of the Amundsen Gulf, pushed to almost certain sinking.

We're learning a lot out here about what we could have or should have done, but in reality what we're doing has never been done. Learning is part of the process—a process that's proving perilous of late. None of our previous expedition experiences, from Paul's row across the Atlantic to my ski to the South Pole and Frank's canoe trip across Canada, were unprecedented. People before us had at least attempted and often completed similar expeditions, and the experiences they gathered proved invaluable to our own preparations. But our attempt to traverse the Northwest Passage by rowboat has never been done before. We're in uncharted waters.

A steely gray wash bleeds into the evening light and paints a gloom on the unfolding scene. By two in the morning, huge chunks of sea ice, some easily as wide as our beach, have appeared out of nowhere and surrounded the island. "I think it's the sea ice being blown in from Franklin Bay," Frank says.

One towering giant, maybe fifty feet high, pushes itself up onto a small rock outcrop just offshore, and before long we're encircled by a horde of icy marauders looking to breach our island defense. We haul the *Arctic Joule* as high up on the beach as our winch system will allow and wait. By morning our boat is encased in a slushy porridge with larger chunks of ice groaning.

We set up our tent a short distance above the beach, on a grassy bench, and monitor the boat around the clock. It's barren and desolate on this little island but, for the moment, we're safe and out of the storm.

THE YEAR WAS 1997, and my friend Jerome Truran and I were debating what represented an adventuring world first, still unachieved as of today. Jerome is a world-class paddler and had been part of a South African team that made the first source-to-sea descent of the Amazon River in 1985–86; his opinion holds a lot of sway for me. He was convinced that a traverse of the infamous Northwest Passage under human power in a single season lay at the top of the adventure-prize tick list, and I wholly agreed. "But there's just one problem, Jerome," I pointed out. "There's too much ice up there to get across." At the time, I was right; the Northwest Passage was perpetually ice-choked, and a window of navigable open water in its channels was so fleeting that a single-season traverse under human power could never be achieved. But the seed of an idea was planted.

In the summer of 2007, I traveled to the Canadian High Arctic as part of an expedition to walk the desolate shores of King William Island on the Northwest Passage. It was here, just off its northwest shore in 1846, that Sir John Franklin's ships *Erebus* and *Terror* became trapped in sea ice and sank. All 129 officers and crew of the expedition perished. The rocky beaches of King William Island still hold clues to what happened to these men, and we ventured there in hopes of better understanding their story. We stepped into an environment pristine and raw, a world where bitter winds roar uninterrupted across a landscape of rock and ice and where life hangs by a thread. Local Inuit historian Louie Kamookak took us to a small islet off the coast and showed us human bones scattered in the gravel and scrub. We saw flat rock rings hinting at possible graves, and a human skull sitting in a bed of sand, untouched and anonymous. By this time, Jerome's idea had sat with me for a decade and I'd become fascinated by the Northwest Passage and the stories of its exploration. I walked the shoreline and gazed out over the shallow waters of Simpson Strait—the narrowest point of the Northwest Passage, separating King William Island from the mainland—and thought about the history of this region.

Less than two centuries ago, the Arctic was considered *terra incognita,* a wild and unforgiving landscape oblivious to the goings-on of the rest of the planet; to a great extent, it remains that way today in our collective consciousness. But in 2007, when I spied a small piece of white Styrofoam washed up high on the shoreline, I recognized that this was no longer the case. Over the last thirty years, the Arctic has warmed more than any other region on earth—in the first half of 2010, air temperatures there were a staggering 4 degrees Celsius (7 degrees Fahrenheit) warmer than measured between 1968 and 1996—causing dramatic changes to sea ice, snow cover, and permafrost. The delicate balance that defined Arctic ecology was being shaken to its core as the harsh Arctic climate rapidly evolved from a measure of strength to a measure of fragility.

After returning from King William Island, I learned that sea ice in the Arctic had declined to an unprecedented level over the summer—a full 23 percent less than the previous benchmark, which had been set in September 2005. The news came as a shock to me, but not to the climate scientists studying it. Just a few months earlier, the Intergovernmental Panel on Climate Change (IPCC) had predicted in their fourth report that climate change would cause severe melting of Arctic sea ice. An internationally accepted authority on climate science backed by 195 governments worldwide, the IPCC has been making it clear since its inception in 1988 that the "warming of the climate system is unequivocal."

THE FIRST SCIENTIFIC inklings that burning carbon could contribute to disastrous heating of the earth's atmosphere surfaced in the late 1950s, but it didn't hit world consciousness until June 23, 1988, when James Hansen, then director of NASA's Goddard Institute for Space Studies, testified to the U.S. Senate that he had "99% confidence" in "a real warming trend" caused by human activity. The soft-spoken American, an internationally respected climate scientist, instantly thrust the concept of global warming into the public consciousness. Newspapers, television, and radio buzzed with the new theory. Political pundits mused on the theory's validity and debated solutions. The air rang out with calls for action from an invigorated environmental community. In an unorthodox move after a year of hurricanes, earthquakes, droughts, and floods—all predicted outcomes of the climate crisis—the editors of *Time,* the world's largest weekly circulation magazine, declared the first "Planet of the Year" (a substitute for its annual "Person of the Year"), with a headline demanding, "What on EARTH are we doing?"

The same year, the United Nations created the IPCC to advise governments on climate threats. In 1992, leaders from 105 countries gathered in Rio de Janeiro for a world conference, where they pledged their commitment to sustainability and environmental protection. In 1997, the fourth such conference resulted in the groundbreaking Kyoto Protocol, the world's first greenhouse gas emissions treaty. But while it set internationally binding reduction targets, it exempted over one hundred developing countries, notably China and India, both massive emitters of greenhouse gases. Declaring the accord too one-sided, the United States—the world's biggest emitter of CO_2—refused to ratify it. Over the next dozen years, a merry-go-round of global talks produced little more than waffling and hand-wringing. The 2009 UN climate summit in Copenhagen was heralded as the conference that would break the cycle of climate disappointment. After eleven days of difficult negotiations, delegates produced the Copenhagen Accord, in which all the major polluting governments, including the United States and China, committed to emission reductions. But it, too, proved disappointing; because the commitments were nonbinding, no country was forced to take action.

The one lasting result of Copenhagen was the recognition that a 2 degree Celsius cap on rising temperatures by the end of the century would be essential to avoid climate catastrophe. Although it was a positive step, the pronouncement was made amid increasing CO_2 emissions that would make a 2-degree cap all but impossible to meet without shutting down the global economy.[1] This situation provoked the very conservative World Bank to warn, in a 2012 report, that the planet was "on track for a 4° Celsius warmer world [by 2100] marked by extreme heat-waves, declining global food stocks, loss of ecosystems and biodiversity, and life-threatening sea level rise," and noted that "as global warming approaches and exceeds 2°C, there is a risk of triggering nonlinear tipping elements," which would "include the disintegration of the West Antarctic ice sheet leading to more rapid sea-level rise, or large-scale Amazon dieback drastically affecting ecosystems, rivers, agriculture, energy production, and livelihoods. This would further add to 21st-century global warming and impact entire continents."[2]

So although international awareness of the catastrophic impacts of unchecked global warming has grown, there has been little substantive change since the 1988 inception of the IPCC. It's like we're on a comfortable train journey through the countryside but we're ignoring announcements that a bridge is out just a few miles down the track. Back in 2007, the more I learned about climate change, the more mystified I became as to why we were doing nothing about it when just staying the course will bring devastation. At the same time, musing on this as an individual seemed futile. I could ride my bike to work and recycle everything I could get my hands on, but it wouldn't make an ounce of difference without the political will to make large-scale change. How could an individual voice make even a small difference when surrounded by people with deaf ears?

ON A CLOUDY November morning in 2011, Paul Gleeson and I sat in a small café on Commercial Drive, the main artery through Vancouver's hip East Side. Although just of medium height and build, Paul has the good looks and easy Irish lilt that make women swoon. We'd met a couple weeks earlier at an outdoor festival in North Vancouver where we were both presenters, and I learned he was from Limerick, Ireland, my parents' hometown. Paul had rowed the Atlantic Ocean in 2006 in a uniquely designed ocean-rowing vessel that allowed him and his partner, Tori Holmes, to journey for almost three months from the Canary Islands off the coast of Morocco to Antigua in the Caribbean. The possibilities of his voyage intrigued me, but it was only at the end of our meeting that I mentioned my dream of traversing the Northwest Passage under human power in a single season.

"The outlandishness of the idea is its brilliance," I explained. Where just a few years earlier, while debating the next adventuring world first with Jerome Truran, it would have been pointless to consider a human-powered, single-season traverse of the Northwest Passage because of the pack ice, the unprecedented melting of the summer pack ice had changed that. "If one could make it across the Northwest in a single season, in a rowboat, it would scream to the profound effects climate change is having on the Arctic." With feigned enthusiasm, I suggested to Paul that maybe we could team up to do that. It would be a seamless fit—the achievement of a world first because of a climate-changed world.

"Just tossing the idea out," I said, my words trailing off into the buzz of café chatter. Paul smiled and nodded but otherwise showed little response. I read his coolness as polite disinterest and forgot all about my suggestion until I got an excited call from him a week later. "I've thought of nothing else," he exclaimed. "Let's do this!"

AS I DISCOVERED in 2009—when a team comprising me and two teammates, Ray Zahab and Richard Weber, broke the world record for the fastest unsupported trek from Hercules Inlet, at the edge of the Antarctic continent, to the geographic South Pole—an adventure has an unparalleled ability to capture world attention. Back then, we used satellite technology to maintain a virtual connection with the world over the course of our 660-mile journey. We reached the South Pole on January 7, 2009, after a traverse of 33 days, 23 hours, and 55 minutes, breaking the world record time by over 5 days. "Bacon, Butter Fuel Fastest South Pole Trek" read the newswire headline, using our unconventional diet to help us garner 1.5 billion media impressions on the journey. If a team could make it across the Northwest Passage in a single season in a rowboat, it would capture world attention—and what better way to make a statement about climate change than to do something that was only possible because of climate change?

Paul's phone call changed my world. We began planning immediately, quickly deciding on a four-man team, which would create the optimal balance of power output to boat size, and we could each go about choosing a teammate to join us. I asked my friend Frank Wolf, adventurer and documentarian, and Paul asked his friend and fellow Irishman Denis Barnett. Truth be told, Denis had heard about the expedition planning before Paul could get a call out. He'd desperately wanted to do an expedition for years and fired off a preemptive text to Paul with three simple words: "I need this!"

With a team formed, we set a start date of July 1, 2013, leaving a little over eighteen months to prepare. The cost of the expedition far exceeded any previous adventure any of us had undertaken, with the bulk of funds going to a fully kitted, custom-built, four-man ocean rowing boat. We waded into a quagmire of sponsorship solicitation while balancing our time with the real-life responsibilities of full-time work, staying fit for the trip, and, for me, being a husband and father. Life suddenly became very busy.

The spring and summer of 2012 were a flurry of activity. We spent countless hours researching potential partners and crafting enticing proposals for them. Our hopes grew when a company entertained our proposal and were quashed when they dismissed it. Our fervor in the face of continual rejection seemed obsessive, but we marched on to the beat that we were going to do this thing "come hell or high water."

The summer of 2012 changed everything in the Arctic. On September 16, the Arctic sea ice melted to 1.32 million square miles, an all-time low, about 290,000 square miles less than the previous record, set in 2007. The staggering decline sent the scientific community into a tailspin. No models had predicted a decline greater in area than France, and it left climate scientists in a state of shock.

The timing of our expedition appeared to be perfect, yet a full year after Paul and I had met in that café on Commercial Drive, we were no further along financially than we had been then. To have a boat ready for the summer of 2013, we needed to start building immediately. "We need to expose a little skin," Paul said frankly. "I think we have to put in a little of our own money to get the boat started." We passed the proverbial donation hat and construction began.

By mid-February 2013 we were again out of funds, deeply in debt and seemingly out of luck. For the first time in our planning, the prospect of postponing the expedition to 2014 started to creep into our conversations. Our boat builder halted construction while awaiting another installment, with the boat a mere shell of a hull. A malaise fell over the team.

Our rescue came in the form of a casual comment from Denis Barnett's girlfriend, Niamh Cunningham, when she offered to introduce us to an old friend who now headed up a renewable energy company in Ireland. "Mainstream Renewable Power would be a perfect fit for you lads," she said. "I've known Eddie since I was a kid. He's the dad of my best friend growing up." Niamh's words lit up our hopes like a rescue flare. The light faded quickly into the dark fear of yet another rejection. But it refused to die completely, and within a week we'd spoken with Eddie O'Connor, Mainstream's CEO, and learned of his passion to combat climate change. "He's going to give our proposal some serious thought," Paul said. "He'll get back to us soon."

My wife, Nicky, woke me in the early morning hours of February 27, 2013. "It's Paul on the line," she yelled from the kitchen. "You gotta take the call."

"Hey, Paul, what's up?" I said groggily, a little confused.

"Bad news," he replied. "I got word from Eddie."

"I expected as much," I replied, disappointed but not surprised.

"Looks like you'll be missing your family this summer, Kev," Paul continued. "We're going to the Northwest Passage. *Eddie's on board!*" An ungodly scream erupted from the phone. I was left speechless. We were heading north.

From then on, everything turned into a blur. Our boat builder, Robin Thacker, had been patient with us throughout the sponsorship journey and kept us abreast of the critical milestones he needed to reach in order to have the boat ready for departure in early July. Aware of our financial woes, he remained focused even in the face of almost certain termination. But now it was game time. He began working around the clock and the boat began to take shape. Cabins were built, hatches sealed, and critical equipment installed. The list of technical requirements for our boat was as long as it was unknown. The boat was one of a kind, and Robin orchestrated everything.

Robin Thacker was first recommended to us by a friend, the international adventurer Colin Angus, who described a spirited kayak builder with a keen eye for detail. Thacker had recently sold his kayak business and was eager to take on a new challenge. "He's meticulous and energetic," Colin said. When we met Robin for the first time, he was dressed in oversized jeans, a hip graphic T-shirt, and a trucker hat that made him look half his age. Fascinated by our unique project, he starts generating ideas from the get-go. His knowledge of boat building was so exhaustive and his passion for the job so inspiring that even though his workshop was on Vancouver Island, a ferry ride away for all of us, we quickly decided he was the right man for the job. Our anxieties about having to remotely direct him in his work were quickly allayed as he immediately consumed himself in the task. We learned over time to talk with him only when necessary, as his responses often expanded into dissertations on some aspect of the boat build.

"He's one accident away from being a mad genius," Denis quipped. "He sure knows his stuff, though."

Our negotiations with Mainstream included giving them the right to name the boat. At the end of April, they informed us that they'd run a company-wide contest and selected a double

entendre for a renewable energy company heading north—
The Arctic Joule. We were thrilled to see how Mainstream had
embraced us and knew it was all thanks to the confidence of its
cofounder and CEO Eddie O'Connor. O'Connor has been a force
to be reckoned with on the global renewable energy stage, first
founding the Irish wind farm development company Airtricity,
in 1997 and cofounding Mainstream in 2008. "Mainstream is
proud to sponsor this expedition because it draws attention in
a very forcible manner to the disasters of global warming," he
said to us, his passion for combating climate change shining
through. "It allows us to brand our company with courage. It
allows us to put ourselves into the forefront of the struggle to
stop and reverse climate change. It allows us to demonstrate
to the world that there is an answer to global warming—we
don't have to do without electricity, we don't have to do without
energy, we can have that energy supplied by renewable pow-
ers. That's why it's very important to us as a solar and wind
company."

IT'S JUNE 28, 2013, and we're set to depart. The last two
months have flown by in a blur of activities, from acquiring the
right food, equipment, and clothing to making final tweaks
to the *Arctic Joule* and testing gear to make sure it all works.
The time comes to accept that we've done everything we can
and get on with the job. *The Arctic Joule* sits adjacent to my
house atop an extended boat trailer hitched to Denis's truck.
We've had it shrink-wrapped for the journey north, and my
two daughters—Caitlin, nine, and Arianna, seven—are having a field day doodling flowers, shamrocks, spiral swirls, and
a confused-looking pig on the clean white plastic. Around the
bow I discover a sketch of two polar bears with speech bubbles

above them, one saying, "I'm hungry" and the other saying, "I smell chubby men."

I'm the only team member with children, and my guilt for leaving them this summer weighs heavily on me. About a month earlier, while picking them up from school, one of Caitlin's best friends ran up to me, tugged my jacket, and asked, "Is it true you're going to die?" I laughed out loud and dismissed her question with a simple "No, no, of course not," but her words hung with me. Was this the schoolyard talk? Were parents making such insinuations? Later that night, I asked Caitlin about it and she dismissed it lightheartedly. "I know you'll be okay, Daddy," she said with the confidence only a child can convey. She even sounded proud.

Traversing the Northwest Passage has been a dream of mine since long before my daughters were born, and now I have an opportunity to pursue it. Several people have suggested I forgo it because of my kids, but I believe children learn and develop through the guidance and actions of their parents. My pursuit of a cherished dream, no matter how odd or meaningless it seems to some, is important not only to me. I hope it will also instill in my kids the belief that they can go after their dreams as well. Some day my daughters will come to me with their own ambitions and aspirations and I'll be able to say, "I followed my dreams. You should too."

THE DRIVE FROM Vancouver to Inuvik is just shy of the distance from Vancouver to Toronto, a 2,500-mile straight shot north that provides a sobering reminder of Canada's vast size. Our route travels north up Highway 1 to the city of Prince George, smack dab in the center of British Columbia. From there it's up the Alaska Highway to Fort Nelson—a remote section of road affording sightings of bear, buffalo, and moose around virtually every bend—and on to Whitehorse, the "big city" gateway to the mighty Yukon.

Pushing ever northward, our route takes us into Klondike Gold Rush history as we pay a visit to Dawson City, Yukon, and the terminus of our blacktop. The final section of our route begins a few miles shy of this bustling little tourist town. The infamous Dempster Highway is a 457-mile tire-eating, vehicle-destroying gravel and slate road that pushes boldly north through the mountains and wilderness of the Canadian subarctic to the Arctic Ocean. We later hear that our single flat tire and a punctured power steering column is the Dempster taking it easy on us.

On our drive, I spend countless hours reading Pierre Berton's *The Arctic Grail: The Quest for the North West Passage and the North Pole,* where I find something I've intuitively known all along—that the explorers associated with the hunt for the Northwest Passage are a proverbial who's who of Canadian history, the forefathers of a nation, the names that every Canadian schoolchild recognizes as their own. The quest for the Northwest Passage may have been an adventure saga like no other, but it's also the story of Canada. One of the first explorers to look for the Northwest Passage was Frenchman Jacques Cartier, who in 1535 ventured upriver to the Iroquoian fortified village of Hochelaga. As a Montreal boy, I know the story well, but I'd had no idea he thought the major set of rapids south of the island was all that barred him from reaching the Orient. He would name the spot La Chine, the French for "China," today the town of Lachine, Quebec—my birthplace.

For Canadians, the name Hudson is as iconic as it gets. It's not only the name of the vast inland sea of Hudson Bay in northeastern Canada, but also because the Hudson's Bay Company, now a department store known as The Bay, is the oldest commercial corporation in North America. Back in 1610, when he sailed into the bay that now bears his name, Henry Hudson was convinced he had found the Northwest Passage. His crew were less convinced, and after spending an icy winter locked in the ice, they mutinied and headed for home. Hudson, his teenage son, and seven crew members were set adrift in an open rowboat and never seen again.

What I find bewildering about this story is that not only was Hudson's mutinous first mate, Robert Bylot, pardoned for his actions, when by the laws of the day he should have been hung, but five years later he was granted an expedition of his own. The name Bylot may not be familiar to most Canadians, but William Baffin, the name of his sea pilot and namesake of Baffin Island and Baffin Bay, sure is. Captain George Vancouver explored the Pacific coast of North America in the late 1700s in search of the Northwest Passage. The Dempster Highway crosses the Mackenzie River, discovered by Alexander Mackenzie when he went looking for an inland route to the Pacific. Every way you turn in Canada there's evidence that the quest for the Northwest Passage shaped the country into what it is today.

Putting Berton's book down, I take a deep breath and stare out at the open expanse of green-brown tundra rolling to the horizon. Paul's at the wheel focused on the road, and the rest of us are sprawled around the truck quietly locked in our thoughts. Stunted spruce and arctic willow border our gravel track, confining us to the only straight line that exists in this seemingly limitless landscape. What have we gotten ourselves into? The history of the Northwest Passage reads like a litany of tragic efforts at one-upmanship and woe. Only a couple hours out of Inuvik and the start of our expedition, I wonder if we'll face the same.

2

IT BEGINS

IT'S DIFFICULT TO IMPRESS UPON people to the south how deeply the changes affecting the Arctic will affect them personally, but those who have lived in the North all their lives understand the scope of the changes implicitly. Just before setting off, Frank and I had the opportunity to speak with the current mayor of Inuvik, former premier of the Northwest Territories Floyd Roland. An Inuvialuk by blood, Roland stands well over six feet tall and is a giant among his people. He is a natural-born communicator who is at ease discussing the region he's lived in his whole life. "In a younger day, I didn't fully understand what they were trying to say," he began, referring to the Elders when he was growing up. "So when the men would gather around the fire and have some tea and start talking, they'd say the weather is changing. And as a young boy I'd look up to the sky and think, 'Is it going to rain tomorrow?' It's now that I realize that they were remarking on their history and how the weather has changed."

The section of the Mackenzie River down to the Beaufort Sea, the part we're navigating, is where Roland has witnessed major change since his boyhood. "My father and mother would go out to the cabin and spend what we call freeze-up out there. They would go up by boat and then they would come back in by snow machine. You were pushing it if you went out in mid-September because you had ice forming in the small creeks and sometimes in the bay. A month later, in the middle of October, they'd come in by snow machine crossing those very channels and rivers. Nowadays you can still get to the cabin by boat in October, so there has been change."

For Roland, the question is not whether climate change is happening; he's seen that firsthand. "We've seen lots of land sloughing over the last eight or ten years." he says. "Because of the longer warming trends, it has allowed the surface to melt more far down ... melting more of the permafrost."

Permafrost is perennially frozen soil that has remained below the freezing point for two or more years; it covers about a quarter of exposed land in the northern hemisphere. The melting of permafrost is of huge concern for accelerating climate change because of the release of methane frozen within it. Methane is a powerful greenhouse gas, and researchers estimate that the amount currently locked in the permafrost is equal to about twice the volume of carbon currently in the atmosphere. Eddie O'Connor spelled it out clearly to us before we left: "With the Arctic ice gone, the permafrost is going to melt, and if the permafrost melts there will be a vast release of methane, that CH_4 gas, into the atmosphere. This CH_4 gas is thirty times more effective as a greenhouse-forcing gas than CO_2, so we're headed for almost complete meltdown in our way of life if the permafrost were to melt."

Before we departed Inuvik, Floyd Roland toured us around the community and showed us how buildings there had begun to settle due to the melting of the permafrost. Buildings throughout the North are typically raised up on wooden posts driven deeply into the frozen earth. The structures remain intact and stable as long as the ground remains frozen, but once the permafrost begins to melt, the wood posts start to rot and the buildings settle. Wood posts are now being replaced by concrete all around Inuvik to deal with this problem.

The problem recently manifested in a much more dramatic way in Siberia. Methane comes from the microbial decomposition of organic matter within soil once that soil starts to thaw. When permafrost melts, methane is released. In July 2014 a mysterious crater suddenly appeared in the frozen Siberian landscape of Russia's Yamal Peninsula. Images of the yawning hole, over 100 feet in diameter, went viral around the world. Scientists, who had never seen anything like it before and were baffled as to what had caused it, tossed around explanations ranging from meteorites to rogue missiles; there were even whispers of aliens among those so inclined. The solution to the mystery was published in an August 2014 article in *Nature* magazine, which noted, "Air near the bottom of the crater contained unusually high concentrations of methane—up to 9.6%—in tests conducted at the site on 16 July, says Andrei Plekhanov, an archaeologist at the Scientific Centre of Arctic Studies in Salekhard, Russia. Plekhanov, who led an expedition to the crater, says that air normally contains just 0.000179% methane." Plekhanov's report stated that "as temperatures rose..., permafrost thawed and collapsed, releasing methane that had been trapped in the icy ground."[1] Geochemist Hans-Wolfgang Hubberten of Germany's Alfred Wegener Institute for Polar and Marine Research explained that "gas pressure increased until it was high enough to push away the overlaying layers in a powerful injection, forming the crater."[2] In other words, the melting permafrost released so much methane, it blew out the hole. Scientists had never before postulated such enormous releases of methane gas.

On the other side of the Arctic, in northern Alaska, the permafrost has been warming at about one-tenth of a degree Celsius per year since roughly 2005. Vladimir Romanovsky, a professor at the University of Alaska and head of the Global Terrestrial Network for Permafrost, noted in a *Tech Times* article that "when we started measurements it was –8°C, but now it's coming to almost –2.5°C on the Arctic coast... It is unbelievable—that's the temperature we should have here in central Alaska around Fairbanks, but not there."[3] Romanovsky expects permafrost in parts of Alaska to start thawing by 2070. "It was assumed it would be stable for this century but it seems that's not true anymore."[4]

In addition, scientists have expressed concern that methane may be bubbling up from undersea permafrost in the shallow seas of the Russian Arctic. At the same time, a major new study led by San Diego University suggests that large amounts of methane are escaping from the ground during the Arctic's long cold period, a time when current climate models assume no release at all. Eddie O'Connor's warnings seem to be ringing true. The permafrost is a climate meltdown waiting to happen.

WE'VE SPENT OUR last couple of days scurrying about Inuvik checking final tasks off our to-do list, with the purchase of whiskey high on the list. For some reason, hard liquor costs significantly less here than in Vancouver, so we held off buying it until we arrived. A wee swig of single malt at the end of a hard day's effort is a carrot worth chasing, which could be why plying sailors with grog goes back centuries. We thought of adopting the historical rum ration of the British Navy until we discovered the Brits apportioned a half pint of rum per day to their sailors—almost a liter a day for our team, or one hundred bottles for our estimated seventy-five-day journey. It wasn't all pain and suffering on those legendary British expeditions. We made a more sober decision and went with five bottles.

We also got the boat painted. On the drive up, I etched a shark mouth in the road grime that covered the bow of the *Arctic Joule,* and we liked it so much, I painted it on permanently. She looks fierce now, like a World War II Spitfire, undaunted by what lies ahead.

AS THE *ARCTIC JOULE* slides off the back of the half-submerged trailer, the muddy brown water of the Mackenzie River gently tugs the stern in. Paul has the tether line in hand and pulls the bow in tight to shore. Frank, Denis, and I jump aboard. Paul gives the boat one final push, leaps on deck, and sets us free. It's just before noon on July 5, 2013.

The day is warm and lazy. Mosquitos are the only creatures buzzing in town. In these high latitudes, the summer sun is always up and the rhythm of life responds to the cycle of a season rather than the schedule of a day. We spied a group of very young children playing outside at two in the morning yesterday, as boisterous and carefree as if it were the middle of the afternoon. Our friend Todd McGowan, who joined us in Whitehorse and will now drive our truck and trailer back to Vancouver, stands alone onshore, waving to us in a slow arc. "Good luck, guys," he yells, his voice barely audible over the water. "See you in the fall."

AS WE DRIFT down the mighty Mackenzie River toward the Beaufort Sea, my feelings are more tempered than the growling grin of the *Arctic Joule*. Although I'm elated about realizing my dream, this year has been abnormally cold compared to recent years. If we succeed under such circumstances, our expedition will speak even more loudly to the reality of climate change than we'd imagined; but falling short of our destination could provide climate change deniers with fuel for backlash.

We snake our way down the Mackenzie's turbid waters, an impenetrable wall of green atop the river's freshly eroded banks. It's hovering near 30 degrees Celsius today— 86 degrees Fahrenheit—and cold and ice are the furthest things from my mind. Cooking in the heat, I strip off my jacket to my thermal top. Paul's been rowing bare-chested for the last half hour. We've fallen into rowing shifts of four hours on and four hours off, with Paul and I starting things out. By the end of my first four hours, my body is screaming at me for spending far more time planning this expedition than training for it. My hands are blistered and my backside sore. We trade shifts with Frank and Denis and row continuously for the next twenty-seven hours until we reach the end of the Mackenzie River Delta, where it opens onto Kugmallit Bay and the Beaufort Sea.

"At this rate we'll be in Pond Inlet before we know it," Paul jokes, knowing full well we've been nudged along by the current. But we've made excellent time, traveling roughly eighty-five miles since we started. The riverbank to the east has risen sharply and built to a high point of land in the area. "Fancy we pull ashore and take a gander on what's ahead?" Paul continues, gesturing over his left shoulder.

I'm sitting in the rowing position closest to the bow and Paul is right in front of me. "Good idea," I say.

Kugmallit Bay is very shallow in parts and route-finding can be tricky, so this hilltop view may prove helpful. Paul pulls his right oar inward across his lap so it won't catch the water, lets go, and leans back. He grabs the steering wheel, which sits on deck between our rowing positions on the port side of the boat, and spins it a full rotation to the left. We immediately bank hard to starboard, track straight for shore, and slide up against a small section of sandy beach. Denis has scrambled up on deck and is standing on the perforated metal gunwale on the starboard side with the anchor in hand. We have gunwale platforms attached to both sides of the boat, fore and aft, allowing us to walk around it without much trouble. Denis lobs the anchor to shore, where it sinks deeply into the sand.

It's a short scramble to the ridge, but the ground is steep and rutted with a mix of low-lying grass and exposed dirt. Shoots of purple arctic lupine erupt everywhere and tremble with the wind. The broken ground appears to have been disrupted in the recent past, and it dawns on me that this may be the slope Floyd Roland described as a steep hill bank at the mouth of the delta that had seen recent landslide activity.

The air has cooled and a strong breeze blows in from the sea. I'm happy I put my fleece jacket back on before stepping off the boat. A ground squirrel sits on the ridge, motionless, inquisitive about the interlopers, then disappears as we approach. Swarms of mosquitos rise from the tundra in a seemingly hopeless attempt to reach us, but incredibly, some of them do. "We're picking up a few lady friends," Paul says. "Not my type, though," he adds, laughing. Paul's easygoing and always looks for the good side of things rather than the bad. He struggles a bit as he climbs the slope, an injured hip giving him some trouble. He underwent a hip operation just under a year ago and his surgeon explained he'd need a new hip soon. "My other hip is deteriorating as well," he told me matter-of-factly, but he doesn't allow it to bring him down. "I'll ease off the running and do more biking instead." He continues to the top of the bank without complaint. He's exactly the sort of even-keeled teammate you want on a trip like this.

I gaze out across the myriad channels of the Mackenzie Delta and see the muddy waters of Canada's longest river extending to the horizon. I was hoping to see some hint of Herschel Island from here, but for all my straining I see nothing. It was just east of this old whaling station, at King Point, where in 1905 the great Norwegian explorer Roald Amundsen moored for the winter after transiting though the Northwest Passage, snatching the prize that had eluded the British for over three centuries.

ROALD AMUNDSEN'S MOMENTOUS journey across the Northwest Passage was as inauspicious as it was lean. He was underfunded and deeply in debt when he and his six crew members boarded his tiny, forty-seven-ton, square-sterned sloop, the *Gjøa,* and literally stole away from Oslofjord, Norway, in the middle of the night to avoid creditors. It was

June 16, 1903, and Amundsen and his crew charted a journey virtually identical to the route Sir John Franklin had taken six decades earlier, except for one crucial turn. He, like the famed British explorer, rounded the southern tip of Greenland and headed up its west coast, crossing Baffin Bay and passing through Lancaster Sound, the gateway to the Northwest Passage, so named by William Baffin almost three centuries earlier. He then voyaged westward, through Barrow Strait to Beechey Island, where he found evidence of Franklin's expedition, including the three grave sites marking the first lives lost from that crew.

Amundsen found an ice-free Peel Sound, as Franklin had, and headed south through Franklin Strait to the northern tip of King William Island. There his route and Franklin's diverged. Franklin had turned right and headed down the west side of King William Island, sailing directly into the path of the huge and perennial ice stream that pours down from the Beaufort Sea. His ships, *Erebus* and *Terror,* became inextricably locked in the great morass of ice, upward of one hundred feet thick in places, and he and his crew were never seen again. He was traveling by navigational charts indicating that King William Island was not an island but an extension of the Boothia Peninsula, and he had turned right because he thought he couldn't turn left.[5]

Amundsen knew otherwise. The thirty-plus expeditions sent out in search of the missing Franklin expedition had charted much of the Canadian archipelago and showed that King William Land was in fact an island. Amundsen turned left and navigated the *Gjøa* through the shallow waters on the east side, using the island itself as protection from the great polar pack to the west. He discovered a perfectly sheltered bay at the southeast corner of the island, which crew member Godfred Hansen described as "the finest little harbor in the world." Amundsen and his crew named it Gjøahavn—today's Gjoa Haven—and remained anchored there for two winters.

On August 13, 1905, Amundsen continued west through Queen Maud Gulf, Dease Strait, and the gulf that now bears his name, and on the morning of August 26 he was awakened by his second-in-command, Helmer Hanssen, crying out, "Vessel in sight, Sir!" When the *Charles Nansen* from San Francisco encountered the Norwegian vessel, its captain, James McKenna, exclaimed to Amundsen, "I am exceedingly pleased to be the first one to welcome you on getting through the Northwest Passage."

The meeting between Amundsen and McKenna hints at what mariners of the time considered the Northwest Passage. Today, it's defined as a sea route through the Arctic Ocean along the northern coast of North America through the Canadian Arctic Archipelago, with the start and finish identified as those points where the Arctic Circle meets the Atlantic and Pacific oceans. But Amundsen seemed to think otherwise. Upon spying the *Charles Nansen,* which had come from the Pacific, he believed he had conquered the Passage. In his diary he wrote, "The Northwest Passage was done. My boyhood dream—at that moment it was accomplished. A strange feeling welled up in my throat; I was somewhat overstrained and worn—it was weakness in me—but I felt tears in my eyes."

After mooring at King Point and preparing the *Gjøa* for its third winter, Amundsen wanted to share his news of his success with the world. "I was wild with eagerness to get to a telegraph office and send the news to the world of our success in conquering the Northwest Passage."[6] He accompanied the mail run from Herschel Island to the nearest telegraph post, at Eagle, Alaska, some five hundred miles south. Since he'd snuck out of Norway with creditors on his tail, he was now penniless and was forced to send his telegraph collect, creating such confusion that the press received his news before King and country. On December 6, 1905, the *San Francisco Chronicle* headline trumpeted, "Traverses the Northwest Passage: Captain Amundsen Claims to Have Found the Magnetic Pole in the Steamer Gjoa."

We chose the Mackenzie Delta as our starting point because Amundsen and the rest of the world seemed certain that he'd succeeded in crossing the Northwest Passage when he reached it. We will attempt to travel from the Mackenzie Delta through the archipelago to the eastern portal at Lancaster Sound, which we've chosen as our terminus because this opening into Baffin Bay has been recognized as the gateway to the Northwest Passage ever since William Parry sailed through it in 1819. By modern standards, our route may not be considered a full transit of the Northwest Passage, but it represents the crux. Getting to Lancaster Sound at the eastern side or Mackenzie Delta at the western side was not a mystery to the mariners of yore; the puzzle always lay in between. This is the passage we will attempt.

I stand atop the windswept knoll and stare out at Beaufort Sea. Amundsen traveled these waters just over a century ago, a blip on the historical clock, but in such a short time the Arctic has undergone enormous change. What does its future hold now?

A FEW MONTHS before leaving on our journey I had the opportunity to formally present our expedition to delegates at *The
Economist* magazine's Arctic Summit in Oslo. I traveled there
with trepidation, anticipating pushback on my belief that climate change was profoundly affecting the Arctic. The attitude
of the Canadian government at the time—that climate change
was still in question and, if it did exist, was not as serious as
was being portrayed—shaped this perception, along with the
fact that *The Economist*'s readership skews conservative. If
political or corporate climate change skeptics were to be found,
I assumed they'd be at this summit.

Nothing could have been further from the truth. The Arctic
Summit brought together over two hundred scientists, policy-
makers, industry leaders, and environmentalists from around
the globe and, regardless of the diversity of their mandates, all
delegates agreed on three things—climate change was happening, it was being caused by humankind, and it was profoundly
affecting the Arctic. The clarity of the vision buoyed my spirits,
but the overall message from the summit, that climate change
was happening faster than anyone expected, shocked me.
Climate scientists, still reeling from the previous summer's
lowest-ever-recorded seasonal ice cover, lamented that this
low level hadn't been forecasted by their models for decades to
come. Predicting that the Arctic would become ice-free in the
summer much sooner than anticipated, they expressed their
feelings that all bets for the Arctic were now off. One scientist,
speaking off the record, believed it might happen this decade.
Yet back in Canada, Leona Aglukkaq, the Conservative government's environment minister, described as "debatable"
whether the Arctic was warmer.[7] The government's reluctance

to act implied its concern that recognizing the dangers of continued carbon emissions would have undesirable consequences for the oil industry, the backbone of the Canadian economy. Like a smoker craving one more cigarette, the government seemed to favor short-term satisfaction over long-term health.

WE SCRAMBLE DOWN our slope and back to the boat. Wind is rippling the water in Kugmallit Bay. We can see no hint of the shoals that lie below it from our high point, but we know they're out there. The orange river marker we spied just downstream on our approach appears to indicate the point where we need to turn up coast. The village of Tuktoyaktuk is only twenty-five miles from here. We should be there in no time.

The Mackenzie carries mountains of silt in its waters and deposits much of its load in the delta. Navigation can be tricky through these murky waters, as sandbars lurk everywhere. Much of the delta, hundreds of square miles in area, is less than four feet deep. Our magic number is two feet; anything less and we're grounded. And grounded we are, almost immediately after we pass the orange marker.

"Christ, maybe we should have gone down that other channel," Denis yells, pointing to a waterway closer to shore. We all pull on our dry suits and jump in the water. We're a couple of miles offshore and it's only a foot deep. With Paul and Frank at the bow and Denis and me at the stern, we push the boat back and forth until it slides off the shoal. Frustrated, Denis shouts, "Unbelievable!" He's the biggest member of the team, and his barrel-chested physique cuts the build of a rugby player more than an endurance athlete. He's quick to express his opinion, unlike the rest of us, who tend to hold our tongues until pressed, but there's charm in his forthrightness. Denis, a comedian at heart and one of the funniest people I've ever met, is eager to show he belongs. Frank and I have participated in numerous major expeditions in the past, several of which we've done together, and we're best of friends; we each know exactly how the other will react in a given situation. Paul is a new teammate for both of us, but his significant experience of rowing across the Atlantic Ocean mixed with his even-keeled personality makes for little concern. Denis is the unknown. He's the newbie on the team, as he put it himself, and at thirty-one, he's also the youngest member of the team. (I'm forty-seven, Frank's forty-two, and Paul's thirty-seven.) When Paul first suggested Denis as our fourth teammate, I was very unsure. If it had not been for their close friendship, I likely would have been unreceptive to the idea. On an adventure like this, bringing on someone so untested could be a disaster waiting to happen, but we're here now and I'm watching intently to see how Denis will bear up under the reality of the expedition.

The water's like soup; it's impossible to judge what's beneath it. Rowing proves hopeless as we blindly bump from one sandbar to the next, with all four of us jumping in the water to pushing the *Arctic Joule* off again each time. "I'm just going to pull her," Frank says as he grabs the bowline and starts to haul from the front.

Denis puts on his PFD, attaches the bowline to the back of it, and starts to haul the boat the way one might a sled. "It's like you're walking a large dog," I shout to him. He looks back at me with a bemused expression. I can't tell whether he's angry or amused. But walking in front of the boat allows us to discover sandbars before the boat does, so we resign ourselves to hauling rather than rowing. It takes us hours to negoti- ate the delta, but eventually the water deepens and we begin to row again. By one in the morning Sunday, the sun is shin- ing brightly over a calm sea and we are moving up the coast toward Tuktoyaktuk. Our world is bathed in a radiant yellow light usually identified with sunsets, but up here sunsets last all night long. A caribou runs along the shoreline oblivious to us, shaking its head back and forth in a futile attempt to keep the mosquitos at bay. Listening to my iPod, which is randomly pulling songs from a two-thousand-plus shuffle mix, Stan Rogers's "Northwest Passage" comes up to play. I row in calm disbelief as the anthem unfolds and Rogers, a capella, sings of his desire to trace that passage, "to find the hand of Franklin," who sought to do the same.

A sense of contentment washes over me. Tuktoyaktuk lies just ahead. If we can maintain this pace, we'll be there by early afternoon.

3

STORMY WEATHER ON
THE BEAUFORT SEA

I WAKE WITH A START as the *Arctic Joule* heaves hard to starboard. I look at my watch: it's 5:15 a.m., only an hour since I lay down. Paul isn't moving. Another jolt and the boat heels over again.

"It's getting rough out there," Paul mumbles, rolling slowly over in his sleeping bag.

"Feels like it," I reply. I peer through the plexiglass cabin door and see Frank and Denis rowing intently, faces stern, tempo high. The sea is steep and choppy and the wind is bearing down on us with purpose. It's a far cry from the calm we experienced just a few hours ago. I crack the hatch a couple inches and yell out, "What's up, guys?"

"We're barely moving," Denis responds, clearly frustrated. He continues rowing while speaking and I can hear the effort in his voice. "The wind's picked up, it came out of nowhere."

I pull the hatch closed to prevent sea spray from getting into the cabin and turn the upper and lower handles inward to fully seal it. "We should start getting ready," I say. "We're up in less than an hour." Paul and I roll up our sleeping bags, push them into waterproof stuff sacks, and move them to the back of the cabin. I slip on a pair of fleece pants and jacket, open the rear cabin hatch, and stand up through it. There are two large hatches in the aft cabin. One, which faces the center of the boat, swings like a regular door on vertical hinges; the other, which I'm currently standing in, opens like an operable skylight. Located at the back of the cabin, this one provides access to the rear rudder, which we can raise and lower as needed without having to shimmy around the exterior gunwales of the aft cabin. This proved very handy as we bumped our way over the sandbars yesterday, but it also serves another purpose. Standing hands-free and maintaining my balance by pressing my thighs against the hatch edges, I look back at where we've come from, drop my pants, and start to urinate.

"Careful up there," Paul mumbles. "You don't want to slip, now." His concern is more for my aim than my well-being. "We didn't have that hatch when we rowed the Atlantic," he says, shaking his head as I drop back into the cabin. He's referring to his ocean traverse in 2006. "I had to go out on deck every time, or pee in a bottle in here when it was rough . . . and it was even harder for Tori," he adds, pointing out the obvious issue facing Tori Holmes, his female teammate on the journey.

The Arctic Joule is similar to the boat Paul and Tori used. Both vessels were built from the prototype most commonly used in modern-day ocean traverses, with a closed fore cabin for storage, an open central area for rowing, and a closed aft cabin for crew accommodation. The overall form of the boat makes it stable in big water while still allowing it to self-right if flipped. The hull is made up of fourteen independently sealed storage compartments as well as excellent redundancy in the event of a breach. No boat is unsinkable, but ocean rowing boats, with this type of multi-bulkhead construction, get pretty darn close.

The Arctic Joule, like other boats in its class, is equipped with a water desalinator, which transforms ocean water into fresh drinking water. Our ballast, which is situated along the keel, does double duty as our fresh water supply, and our desalinator keeps it perpetually topped up. Solar panels that cover the top of both the fore and aft cabins and feed into two 12v car batteries below deck power the desalinator and all our other electronic equipment: a navigational computer with two screens and GPS, two satellite phones, a mobile router, two laptop computers, two SPOT Satellite GPS Messenger devices, two cameras, three video cameras, four iPods, an iPad, and a VHF radio. An ocean rowing boat like ours can be fully self-sufficient for months, if adequately provisioned.

Our vessel differs from a regular ocean rowing boat in one fundamental way: it needs to be able to run into things. Unlike on the Atlantic, a vessel on the Northwest Passage will encounter obstacles—shoals, reefs, rocks, and ice—and needs to be extra resilient. We've altered the standard plywood and epoxy lay-up of a regular ocean rowing hull by reinforcing ours with Kevlar and dense foam to provide strength and elasticity in the event of impact. We've made the rudder and keel retractable for the same reason.

"Fancy a cup of scald?" Paul asks, referring to a cup of scald-ing hot tea.

"I'd love one," I say. Both Paul and Denis are from Ireland, and each has a quiver of expressions that routinely fly over my head, even though my parents are both from Ireland, but I catch this one. "You grab the tea bags and I'll put on the water," I say. I open the deck hatch an inch and warn Denis that I'll be opening the door. The stove is just outside the hatch in the footwell and, at the moment, Denis is in the rowing position closest to it. If he's at the start of his drive phase—the moment when his legs are fully bent and he's ready to start pulling back on the oars—the door will hit him when it opens. I need to time it perfectly. "Door opening," I yell through the gap and push it open as Denis slides backward away from me. "Just brewing up a little water," I say to him. A rush of cool air sweeps through the cabin. The gentle ocean surface I was gazing out over a few hours ago is now an angry and frothy chop. I lean out to the left and start pumping the deck pump, which draws fresh water from our ballast tank to a plastic spigot that protrudes out from the front wall of the footwell. The pot is tucked under the spigot neck, and water begins to flow into it. We're using a fully integrated pot-stove system called a Jetboil that is designed to be stable even in heaving seas. I press the auto-ignite button, hear the roar as the stove starts up, and retreat to the cabin.

We've reduced the length of our rowing shifts from four hours to three, which means we're less tired at the end of a session but more rushed during our breaks. Paul and I have just finished our second cup of tea when we realize it's time to head back out. Looking through the plexiglass hatch door, I see Denis stop rowing at exactly the three-hour mark. "He's watching the clock closely," I say out loud. I don't blame him, of course, as time moves much slower for the rower on deck than the rower in the cabin.

BY THE TIME Paul and I take our turn at the oars, the wind and waves have intensified so much that we row for ninety minutes in one position before realizing our efforts are fruitless. The seas are tossing the *Arctic Joule* everywhere, so we throw out the anchor and slip back into the cabin to wait out the weather.

Our cabin is approximately the area of a king-size bed, with marginal headroom; we can sit comfortably at the door side but not the stern. Its height tapers from a high point of 50 inches at the deck door to a low point of 25 inches at the back. The width tapers as well, from 84 inches at the hatch door to 40 inches at the far stern. In this space we store all our personal gear, including sleeping bags and mats, clothes and toiletries, and all the other items we want close at hand, like a book, a journal, a coffee cup and bowl, an iPod, a water bottle, and maybe even a small flask of single malt. Add to this the essential equipment—like the navigation panel, the electrical panel, a fire extinguisher, a large Pelican case with all our communication equipment and a smaller Pelican case with our Nikon D600 SLR, and the huge assortment of cables and plugs that come with everything—and things start to get tight. Arrange all this gear in the periphery of the king-size bed and plunk down four reasonably big guys, unwashed and unkempt, one or two slightly foul and all very tired, and you get a picture of what it's like in our cabin. All four of us are in the cabin only when it's storming outside, so shaking this picture violently in every imaginable direction for hours on end gives a pretty good idea of what it's like on anchor in a storm.

I've fallen asleep through the storm. The only way all four of us can sleep in relative comfort is if one of us sleeps in the opposite direction to everyone else. There's less headroom facing the opposite direction, but I have volunteered for the role knowing full well that the farther away I am from the faces of my snoring teammates, the better off I'll be. I'm not certain how Frank and Denis snagged the premium outer spaces against the cabin walls—those are by far the best positions, as they each have only one person wedged against them—but I can't see them giving their spots up now. From my experience, once sleeping positions in a tent (or in this case a tent-sized cabin) are established, they never change.

Now I awake with a start. Paul and Denis are asleep and Frank's on deck. The wind hasn't diminished and it's clear we're not leaving any time soon. I slip into my dry suit and head outside. The shore's tantalizingly close. I dip an oar into the water to see how deep it is and it hits the sandy bottom almost immediately. "The water's only a couple feet deep," I say to Frank. "You want to head in?"

It's an easy 300-yard shuffle to shore with our dry suits on. The fresh water of the Mackenzie River is warmer and less dense than the salty Beaufort Sea, and floats on top of the saltwater. I bend down and scoop a little water to my mouth. "It's not salty at all," I say to Frank, who's walking beside me. "Where do you think all the sewage from upriver has gone?" he says with a touch of impatience in his voice. Frank is used to moving fast and light on his expeditions and this one is causing him some frustration. He's made a career as an adventurer, undertaking an astonishing fourteen major expeditions since he canoed across Canada in 1995 in a single season, the first time anyone ever accomplished such a journey. He typically journeys by canoe, and I sense already that the size and awkwardness of the *Arctic Joule* is less to his liking than the nimbleness and freedom of a canoe.

The beach is a mix of sand and gravel, with driftwood everywhere. Roald Amundsen commented on the abundance of wood a century ago. We're about sixty miles north of the tree line, so the river has brought it all here. The Mackenzie disgorges seventy-eight cubic miles of water into the Arctic Ocean each year, and with it comes a flotilla of debris. Immense tree trunks are tossed about the shoreline like matchsticks, their roots as wild as the hair of Medusa but petrified and gray as if frozen from a glimpse of themselves. Clusters of pinkish-purple wildflowers called arctic parraya hide in the lee of these reclining giants, defiant in the face of the incessant blow.

"I'll start a fire," Frank says as he rummages about for kindling. I look out to sea and notice Paul and Denis out on deck.

"Hey, guys," I yell, "Come onto shore. We're going to start a fire."

Frank gets a fire going quickly, and it's not long before the boys have joined us and we're all huddled around it waiting for the wind to die. Denis pulls out a pipe, lights it, and draws deeply. He and Paul brought pipes along as a nod to the explorers of yore and have been eager to try them out. The sweet, musty smell of tobacco smoke pulls me back to time spent with my grandfather in Ireland as a child. Paul struggles with his poke and sucks air like a winded sprinter. "It's harder than it looks," he says.

By midafternoon, the wind dies. We have just enough time to pack up, return to the boat, and begin rowing again before it rebuilds. "For Christ's sake," Denis says. "We're never going to make it at this rate."

"How about we try pushing her a bit," I say. "We'll be moving forward at least."

The shoreline is sandy and shallow and lends itself to fairly straightforward walking, even with our behemoth in tow. "Even if we only push at one kilometer per hour," Paul says, feigning enthusiasm, "it'll still give us twenty-four kilometers in a day."

"Yeah, we'll be home by Christmas," Denis says. "Christmas 2015."

And so it goes. We row when we can and push when we can't but keep moving forward regardless, three hours on and three off. On one of the pushing shifts, Denis yells out that he sees a beaver in the water. "Check it out! It's right there in the shallows." Soon we all see it, brown and sleek, looking at us for a moment, slapping its tail, and then it's gone.

"There's no way that can be a beaver," I say, incredulous. "It's gotta be a sea otter or something." It sure looked like a beaver, though.

BY EARLY MONDAY morning we're within sight of Tuktoyaktuk, but the wind has intensified and pushing has become virtually impossible. We've come across a small inlet, its entrance not much more than fifty yards wide at the mouth. It separates us from the far shoreline. We decide to slip into it to find protection. Frank and I jump up onto deck—it has been our pushing shift—and let the wind push the boat into the waterway. Our passage quickly opens up into a series of inter-connected channels running parallel to the shoreline, with a finger of land acting as its breakwater, separating it from the ocean. We maneuver ourselves around a gravel spit and enter a tiny bay with calm water, a welcome change from the rumbling sea we've been facing. The Tuktoyaktuk Peninsula appears impenetrable from its shoreline, but when you venture into it like we have, you realize the landscape is a potted surface of lakes and channels, as much water as solid ground.

"We can never move in this," Frank says as we watch the water being blown into a frenzy. "We're stuck here until this dies." The gravel spit we're behind affords some level of protec-tion, but it's not a place we'd like to stay for any length of time.

"It's a lot calmer over there," I say, pointing to the lee side of the opposite shoreline. "That hill there is acting as a great windbreak."

Frank and I have been doing shifts together since our last wind stoppage, and we set off across the mouth of the inlet to its far side. We ferry the *Arctic Joule* upriver, pointing the bow at a forty-five-degree angle into the onshore wind, and start rowing hard. It appears at first as if we're rowing away from where we want to go, but if we pointed the boat straight at our destination, the wind would push us broadside and force us farther inland. The wind is very strong now and we struggle to maintain our line, but with a final burst of effort we slide into a perfectly protected grassy bay behind a large pingo. The landscape of the Tuktoyaktuk Peninsula is flat except for these distinctive cone-shaped grassy hills. At first glance, they look like miniature volcanoes, but instead of having been created by molten rock pushing up from below, they were formed by expanding ice in a mechanism similar to frost heaving the earth up, but to heights of 230 feet. Pingos are unique to the Arctic and subarctic, with this region of the Mackenzie Delta boasting one of the largest concentrations (some 1,350 examples have been recorded). The big pingo acting as our windbreak sits right at water's edge. On the ocean side, it has been eroded to form a steep cliff of mud and rock, but on the opposite side, where we're anchored now, it's an inviting slope carpeted in arctic flowers and grass.

We're only four and a half miles from Tuktoyaktuk and, incredibly, we can pick up cell coverage from here. It feels strange being holed up in the wilds of the High Arctic knowing full well a polar bear could wander by at any moment yet still be able to surf the net and post to Facebook. But easy communication is an unexpected bonus, and we avail ourselves of the convenience to communicate with friends, family, and the Canadian Ice Service. From the CIS we learn that the pack ice of the Northwest Passage is still well formed just beyond the Tuktoyaktuk Peninsula (only about 125 miles ahead) and the Passage still remains fully blocked between the mainland and Banks Island (another 125 miles farther on). It appears there's no big rush for us to move eastward, and the weather report we've just received supports this.

Thirty-knot easterlies shift to thirty-five-knot northeasterlies and make a gale out of a bluster. We build a fire and we tramp to the top of our pingo, walk the windswept shoreline, and wait. We sleep, we eat, read, sneak a few swigs of whiskey, and wait. Although it's a disheartening start to our adventure, it's not often in our hectic lives that we have nothing to do, so we try to be philosophical about it. We need to be patient and enjoy where we're at. The ice still blocking our route ahead needs a strong wind exactly like this to break it up. The forced break may be a blessing in disguise.

Monday drifts into Tuesday and we're still stuck. Our detailed maps indicate a possible route to Tuktoyaktuk running through a series of semi-protected channels on the lee side of the sandy shoreline to the northeast. The hamlet is tantalizingly close—the roofs of its homes peer at us over the horizon—so we decide to go for it. We start hauling and lining the *Arctic Joule* (pulling it from shore by a rope attached to the bow) along the spongy edge of the channel. But it's not a shallow water edge like on the beach, and we often find ourselves in water too deep to push. After five hours of hard effort we reach a dead end. The channel, blocked with driftwood, is impassable. "If we were in kayaks, we could just bump over that and be in town," says Frank, frustration in his voice. He stares at the channel of open water just a few yards away on the other side of the driftwood dam. We retreat to our pingo shelter.

HAULING THAT BOAT today, I've gained a strange insight into a 150-year-old mystery in Arctic exploration, generated by a grisly discovery on the beaches of King William Island, a large rowboat—27 feet—from the doomed Franklin expedition, laying abandoned, left after being dragged or pushed to that spot. Two skeletons were on the boat, one sitting at the bow, the other sprawled across the stern. All manner of personal items were scattered about the hull, including eight pairs of boots, silk handkerchiefs, hair combs, *The Vicar of Wakefield* and several other books, a shoemaker's box, a wolfskin robe, six oars, two shotguns, and forty-four pounds of chocolate. The boat faces north, on an apparent retreat to the doomed motherships, *Erebus* and *Terror*.

One hundred fifty years later, we are hauling our 2,600-pound, 25-foot oversized rowboat, loaded to the gunnels with gear, clothing, and equipment, including forty-four pounds of chocolate and a couple of shotguns. Although at times the process is fluid and even graceful, mostly it's an unwieldy chore of grunting, dragging and pushing, waist deep in frigid water as we try to tame a ton of fiberglass that wants to go where a thirty-five-knot wind blows it. We're at the mercy of the elements and worn out by our effort. In 1847, Franklin's crewmen were fighting for their lives. The items in the boat represented their last connection to the home they'd left behind. Stranded in one of the most inhospitable environments on the planet, the men were starved, scared, and exhausted. Historians still theorize about what happened on that beach a century and a half ago, but after today, I can tell them exactly what happened—desperation.

DAY THREE AND still no movement. The winds are holding at thirty knots. The weather report today, Wednesday, July 10, 2013, promises an improving trend, but we can expect twenty-knot northerlies through tomorrow, with a sharp drop in temperature and snow flurries. Although we're bearing up well, we're all anxious to get moving. Having Tuktoyaktuk in our sights isn't helping. We knew coming into this adventure there would be times like this, but as with all things conceptual, the reality feels different. Reindeer herder Mikkel Pulk, in Inuvik, wisely said, "You move on the land when the land allows you to move; otherwise, you wait." Patience is gold for an Arctic traveler, so we kill time any way we can.

"Anyone for a game of boules?" Frank asks. "Yeah, sure," Denis says, "if you teach me how to play."

Paul nods agreeably. He'd like to play too.

"Kev?"

"I'm going to hang and write in my journal," I say to Frank. "You'll kill me anyhow."

Frank, a boules enthusiast, brings a set to barbecues, get-togethers, and even on vacations when space allows. The object of the game is to throw or roll heavy balls as close as possible to a small target ball; the one that gets closest to the target ball wins, the reward being to toss the target ball for the next round. Frank didn't bring a boules set on the trip, of course, so the guys make do with sticks and rocks. The lack of the real thing doesn't dampen their enthusiasm, and I hear hollers and laughter as they leap from mound to mound, locked in battle.

It's here, holed up just outside Tuk, that we get our first taste of outside reaction to our efforts. Cell coverage has afforded us an internet connection, and we've discovered a flood of demeaning comments sweeping over our social media sites. The vitriol is shocking. None of us have ever experienced anything like this before.

One blogger, an affirmed climate change denier called Suyts Space, writes "LOL!!! Rowers not really rowing." A tweeter named Cosmoscon sends out a series of nasty tweets like "The #AGW [anti-global warming] morons at @last-first2013 are at it again!" and "No, They're just stupid #AGW cult members." Cosmoscon tags @StevesGoddard in a number of his tweets. Steve Goddard is the pseudonym of an avowed climate change skeptic named Tony Heller, who is recognized as one of the loudest and most listened-to voices questioning climate science. It would not be amiss to describe him as the "grand wizard" of climate denial. He's prolific in his efforts but he has no background in climate science and publishes his opinions in blogs and newspaper articles rather than peer-reviewed scientific journals. By tagging him, Cosmoscon is trying to draw Goddard into the conversation, but he's already there, making his own snide remarks, saying, among other things, "They should change their motto from 'rowing against climate change' to 'slogging against rational thought process.'" But having someone of Goddard's stature following us is not a bad thing. It's kind of like having the international tobacco lobby take interest in a local anti-smoking campaign. It means we're being noticed.

The intention of our detractors is clear: dismiss the message by dismissing the messengers. Most of the comments on social media are supportive, but these negative ones really eat at me. One of Goddard's blog posts suggests that the wind speeds we're posting are exaggerated, even though official weather postings for the region reflect exactly what we're experiencing. He's suggesting we're too timid to move forward. Being mocked and goaded by individuals hiding behind anonymity is frustrating. With so few checks in social media, individuals with the energy and disposition can effectively mislead people with falsehoods and innuendo. It takes all my willpower not to respond, but I recognize that retaliation is victory for trolls.

"I ignore that stuff," Frank says, completely nonplussed. "I can't be bothered with comments like that. I wouldn't even read them." I believe him, and wish I could feel the same way.

BY MIDDAY FRIDAY the wind has eased enough for us to make a move. It's still blowing at fifteen knots, but it's more of a cross-wind now, and it'll be a good test of our capabilities, and the

Arctic Joule's. Frank and I head out from behind the shelter of our pingo and are immediately pushed back by heavy seas. The waves are much bigger than expected, but we're committed now. We struggle to keep the boat at forty-five degrees to the wind in order to sideslip along shore, but after ninety minutes of white-knuckled rowing, we've traveled barely half a mile. "This is hopeless," Frank says. "We should head in and push."

It's too difficult to turn the boat around, so we surf in to shore. "Guys, we're going to need your help out here," I yell. Paul and Denis come up on deck just as we hit the beach. We all jump off the boat—Frank and I taking the bow, Paul and Denis taking the stern—and start hauling. "It's all hands on deck," Paul says, trying to stay upbeat.

Waves crash hard to port and push the *Arctic Joule* on top of us. "Careful you don't get caught under this thing," Denis warns. "This is really dangerous." *The Arctic Joule* weighs over a ton; if thrust up onto us, we'd be crushed. Like circus trainers trying to calm an agitated elephant, we manhandle our behemoth through breaking surf with the greatest of care. It takes us an hour to round a small headland, where the seas lessen and we can row again. The timing is perfect, as rocks had begun to appear in the surf and the *Arctic Joule* was running up hard against them. Finally the homes we've been seeing in the distance for days take shape before us. We slip into a small bay at the south end of town and moor on a pebbly beach.

"Jaysus, we made it," Denis says.

4

TUKTOYAKTUK

IT'S 9:30 P.M. ON FRIDAY, July 12, and we've finally made it to Tuktoyaktuk. The journey from Inuvik took nine days instead of the two we'd expected. We've all been taken aback by the power of the wind and the steepness of the waves. "We didn't have a lot of control out there," Paul says.

As we unload gear from the boat, an RCMP truck approaches and two police officers stride down toward us side by side, faces serious. They look like they mean business. One of them is pulling a notepad out. I feel like we were going to be ticketed, but I can't imagine what we might have done wrong.

"We received a call of a boat in distress," the male officer says.

His female partner has pulled out a small yellow notepad. "Names, please."

It soon emerges that a resident saw us rowing what looked like a disabled boat, and assumed we'd lost a motor and were in distress. I guess ocean rowing boats aren't very common up here. As we explain who we are and why we're here, the officers visibly relax the air of authority they first conveyed. They show genuine interest in our adventure, so we show them around the *Arctic Joule* and explain more about what we're doing and where we hope to get.

"You guys have any weapons on board?" the male officer asks.

"Ah, well, yes," Paul says. "We have two shotguns. But we've all done our gun courses and we're all certified to carry—"

The male officer interrupts him midsentence. "That's fine," he says. "I'm just happy you have a gun." I suspect the Arctic is the only place in Canada where it puts an RCMP officer at ease to know a civilian is carrying a gun.

"Do you know if there's a store open in town?" I ask, hoping we can get some fresh food for the evening.

"The Northern closes at ten p.m.," the female officer says. "You only have a few minutes. We'll give you a lift up if you like."

Paul and Denis head off with the two officers while Frank and I remain on the beach. We've pulled the *Arctic Joule* up against the gravelly shore and anchored her to the trunk of a large driftwood log lying on the beach. It's nearly ten o'clock at night and it's as bright as if it were the middle of the day, but low-lying clouds driven swiftly overhead by a cold Arctic wind create a sense of gloom. The temperature hovers near zero and I move around to stay warm. The gravel shore we're on pushes inland, giving way to a thick carpet of driftwood that sweeps up to a dirt road. I can see the red lights of the RCMP truck as it disappears among buildings to the north.

"So this is Tuktoyaktuk," I say to Frank. "A lot of effort just to get to our start." Tuktoyaktuk was supposed to be the starting point of our expedition, but the only vehicular access to the hamlet is via ice road in the winter. Inuvik was the closest community to Tuktoyaktuk we could drive to, except we've lost a week and a half just getting here.

The name Tuktoyaktuk is an anglicized version of the Inuvialuit place name meaning "resembling a caribou." As legend has it, a woman witnessed a herd of caribou entering the ocean here, where they turned to stone. At low tide, along the shore of town, a reef resembling the petrified animals can be seen. Tuk, as it's most commonly called, was once named Port Brabant but the name reverted back to the traditional Inuvialuit name in 1950, the first Canadian community to do so.

From this distance the hamlet reminds me of many northern communities I've visited. Most of the buildings are single-story, wood-clad structures with metal roofs surrounded by a wide variety of metal containers and drums. You can feel the cold environment through the harshness of the architecture. Utility poles forest the hamlet, and their wires create a web of visual clutter above everything else. It's an unfortunate but unavoidable reality, as burying wires in the frozen soil would be impractical. Buildings sit atop wood or concrete posts driven into the permafrost, ensuring that the warm buildings don't melt the permafrost and compromise foundations.

Paul and Denis arrive back with a cardboard box full of goodies, including burgers and buns, cheese and chips, and a case of Coke. "A junk food feast," Paul says, grinning. Frank whips up a driftwood fire to cook on and we gorge ourselves like wolves at the kill. Rationing when you have to and feasting when you can is de rigueur for an expedition.

An elderly woman walks toward us from the road. Tuk is a sizable town by Arctic standards, with a full-time population of 954, but it's small enough that the bulk of the town likely knows we're here. The woman is smiling when she reaches us. "I saw you coming in," she says. "Where you guys come from?"

"We're from Vancouver," I say, my mouth still half full of food. "We started our trip in Inuvik nine days ago." Her name is Eileen Jacobsen and she's an Elder in town. She and her husband, Billy, run a sight-seeing business. "You should come up to the house in the morning and have some coffee," she tells us.

Our night's sleep in the *Arctic Joule* is fitful; our overindulgence runs through all of us like a thunderstorm. By seven in the morning, even with both hatches open, lighting a match in the cabin would blow us out like dirt from that Siberian crater. The roar of the Jetboil pulls me out. Frank's already up, down jacket on, preparing coffee. "You like a cup?"

IT'S STILL TOO early to drop by Eileen Jacobsen's house, so we walk into town on the dusty main road, our ears assaulted by a cacophony of barking dogs. Dirt is the surface of choice for roads and runways in Arctic communities, as any inflexible surface like concrete would be shredded by the annual freeze–thaw cycle. Most of the town runs the length of a thin finger of land, with the ocean on one side and a protected bay on the other. About halfway down the peninsula, a cluster of wooden crosses rests in a high grass clearing, facing west. We heard about this graveyard in Inuvik. Because of melting permafrost and wave action, it's eroding into the sea, and community members have lined the shore with large rocks to forestall its demise. This entire peninsula will face this threat in the coming years. There's not much land here to hold back a hungry ocean.

We notice an elderly man in a blue winter jacket staring at us a short distance away. He's sitting outside a small wooden house and smiles as we approach. "You guys must be the rowers," he says. "Too windy to be out rowing." His jacket hood is pulled tight over his ball cap and he dons a pair of wraparound shades with yellow lenses that would better suit a racing cyclist than a village Elder. His name is Fred Wolki, and he's lived in Tuk for the last fifty years. "I grew up on my father's boat until they sent me to school in 1944, then I came here."

His father, Jim Wolki, is a well-known fox trapper who transported his pelts from Banks Island to Herschel Island aboard his ship the *North Star of Herschel Island*. Interestingly, we had the *Arctic Joule* moored right beside the *North Star* at the Vancouver Maritime Museum before we left. Built in San Francisco in 1935, the *North Star* plied the waters of the Beaufort Sea for over thirty years, her presence in Arctic waters playing an important role in bolstering Canadian Arctic sovereignty through the Cold War.

"We're curious if things have changed much here since you were a boy," Frank says.

"Well ... it's getting warmer now," Fred says, shaking his head. He gestures out to the water speaking slowly and pausing for long moments between thoughts. "Right up to the 1960s ... there was old ice along the coast ... The ice barely moved ... It was grounded along the coastline." He looks out over the shoreline, moving his arm back and forth. "They started to fade away slowly in the 1960s ... icebergs ... They were huge, like big islands ... They were so high, like the land at the DEW Line station ... over there." He points to the radar dome of the long decommissioned Distant Early Warning Line station that sits on a rise of land just east of us. "It's been twenty years since we've seen one in Tuk." There's no sentimentality or anger in Fred's voice; he's just telling us his story. "It's getting warmer now... Global warming is starting to take its toll... All the permafrost is starting to melt... Water is starting to eat away our land."

I listen to his words, amazed. There's no agenda here, no vested interest, no job creation or moneymaking—just an elderly man bearing witness to his changing world.

We part ways with Fred and continue walking through town. I think about all the rhetoric on our social media sites. Who are these people so fervently denying climate change, and what's their agenda? Have they ever taken the time to speak to people who are seeing the dramatic changes firsthand? What would they say to them? Just as tobacco lobbyists avoid oncology wards, I'm sure our deniers stay far to the south when they spout their uninformed criticisms.

The reality for many deniers is that their rejection of climate science is not only agenda based but fundamentally shaped by their conception of the world. According to Yale University's Cultural Cognition Project, "people with strong 'egalitarian' and 'communitarian' worldviews (marked by an inclination toward collective action and social justice, concern about inequality, and suspicion of corporate power) overwhelmingly accept the scientific consensus on climate change. Conversely, those with strong 'hierarchical' and 'individualistic' worldviews (marked by opposition to government assistance for the poor and minorities, strong support for industry, and a belief that we all pretty much get what we deserve) overwhelmingly reject the scientific consensus."[1]

Political affiliation plays a role as well. An October 2013 Environics poll recorded that only 41 percent of Canadian respondents who considered themselves Conservative Party supporters believed climate change was real, while 76 percent who identified with the Liberal Party believed so.[2] It's even more divided in the United States, with 75 percent of Democrats and liberals believing in the science, compared to a staggering low of 20 percent for Republicans in some regions. Clearly, the way people see their society and how it should be governed influences what they believe.

I suspect this carries across into religious beliefs as well. I grew up Roman Catholic and attended a Jesuit high school, where I was made to understand that the Judeo-Christian tradition sees the earth as having been given to us by God as a place to be used, dominated, and conquered. The Bible makes this very clear: "And God blessed them: and God said unto them, Be fruitful, and multiply, and replenish the earth, and subdue it; and have dominion over the fish of the sea, and over the birds of the heavens, and over every living thing that moveth upon the earth" (Genesis 1:28).

I never took these teachings as literal verse and I realize that most Christians don't either, but there's little doubt this philosophy is entrenched in the values of our post-Enlightenment Western culture, where man is perceived as the pinnacle of life on earth with all else subsidiary to him. We grow, we expand, and we develop. The global economy is based on this fundamental idea.

Yale law professor Dan Kahan, the lead author on the Cultural Cognition Project, explained in *Nature,* "People find it disconcerting to believe that behavior that they find noble is nevertheless detrimental to society, and behavior that they find base is beneficial to it. Because accepting such a claim could drive a wedge between them and their peers, they have a strong emotional predisposition to reject it."[3]

Accepting climate change for what it is would mean fundamentally changing our view of the world. It would mean that the path we've taken to get where we are today was not the *right* path. Over the last two hundred years, since the Industrial Revolution, we have dramatically degraded the world, not out of intentional neglect or malaise, but in the commendable pursuit of a seemingly better life for all. To find out now that the path we've taken in pursuing this goal has been faulty is a hard pill to swallow. For those who find it *too* hard to swallow, ignoring reality may be their only alternative to seeing the foundation of their worldview destroyed.

THE LOCALS IN Tuktoyaktuk are friendly but shy, smiling or waving but otherwise moving along when we approach. We're fortunate to meet up midmorning with Deputy Mayor Darrel Nasogaluak. He echoes Fred Wolki's words: warmer temperatures, accelerated erosion, less ice. Nasogaluak has been in Tuk for almost three decades and chairs the local association of hunters and trappers. "We're having an issue with beaver now, too," he says. "In the last five years, we've really noticed them. They're damming up creeks and there's already a noticeable drop in harvesting whitefish this summer."

"Denis was right," I say. "It *was* a beaver we saw."

We chat with a number of people throughout the day and hear about the new road being built from Inuvik, as well as about the caribou and the beluga hunt. It's beluga season now, but the stormy weather is making it tough for the hunters to head out.

For over five hundred years, the Indigenous people of the Western Arctic have harvested beluga whale in these waters.[4] The hunt represents both an ancestral subsistence food source for the people here and an important cultural tradition. Each summer, hunters and their families from Tuktoyaktuk, Inuvik, and Aklavik travel to traditional whaling camps along the Beaufort Sea coast. Hendrickson Island, just twelve miles off the coast, is one of the most important camps. The hunt, which lasts four to six weeks, takes place during July and early August. It's mid-July now, but the weather has been atrocious for much of the month. With their small window closing, the hunters here are anxious. We sense the urgency among them as we chat, and they likely sense ours, too.

The beluga whales in these waters are part of the Eastern Beaufort Sea population and, as part of their migration, move southwest along the landfast ice edge of the Tuktoyaktuk Peninsula into the shallow waters of the Mackenzie River estuary. Belugas use the shallow waters for molting, calving, and feeding and, despite significant hunting pressure, return to these waters every year. Marine biologists always assumed the warm water of the estuary drew the beluga for calving and because of its abundant food supply, but recently they discovered that the warmer, less saline waters of the delta are connected with significant hormonal changes related to new skin growth. Beluga whales return to the Mackenzie Delta because the water helps them with their annual molt.

The beluga whale is a complex cetacean still not fully understood by scientists. Thousands of years of evolution have shaped the beluga for life around sea ice, and it uses the pack ice both to feed and to hide. A change in sea-ice cover because of climate change will undoubtedly affect these animals; we just don't know how. A 1997 University of Washington study noted that "given the coupling between ice-edge habitat and the prey of many species of Arctic marine mammals, we speculate that a sufficient reduction in the extent of the ice edge, and its associated community, may have deleterious consequences for marine mammals that have evolved with these unique systems."[5] So beluga whale populations are not under threat from the subsistence hunting of Indigenous cultures; it's been going on for centuries and the populations remain strong. The threat to these living symbols of the Arctic are a warming climate, a warming ocean, and an inability to adapt to changes that are happening too quickly.

People often wonder why they should care about the extinction of a species they'll never see, but the extinction of any species, or its serious decline, speaks to deeply disturbing trends. No one knows what the knock-on effect of losing the beluga would be, but it would likely affect the narwhal, the bowhead whale, and the polar bear, which would in turn affect other species, and on and on. It's a classic case of a canary in a coal mine. The world is a web of connections we don't fully understand, and it's naïve to think that the extinction or serious decline of species won't ultimately have catastrophic ramifications just because it's not a species we normally interact with.

WHEN WE FINALLY make it to Eileen Jacobsen's house just after noon, we're welcomed in true Northern style—with an endless supply of coffee and a heaping serving of Arctic char.

"There's more char if you're still hungry," Eileen says as she leans against the stove.

We're all seated around a small kitchen table that opens up to the living room. Her husband, Billy, sits on their large leather couch, engaged by our presence but saying nothing. Eileen is the more talkative of the two.

"You like the fish," she says to Denis, smiling.

"It's delicious," he lies, smiling while checking his head to the side.

"More, then?"

"No, no, I'm good," he stutters. "This is great."

Denis doesn't like fish, and the char has a very rich fishy flavor. He's struggling.

"I'll have more," Paul says.

"Me too," Frank says.

Eileen shows us around her home and explains her and Billy's way of life. They run a small tourism business called Arctic Ocean Tuk Tours. They take visitors out on the Arctic Ocean, share traditional food like muktuk and dry fish, and even take visitors to the community freezer that's built deep into the permafrost. "It's been a slow year so far," she says. "Hopefully the new road will bring more tourism."

It takes a little time to soften up Billy, but with Eileen's banter he eventually joins the conversation.

"You guys aren't heading out in that wind?" he asks, shaking his head. He has the slow speech cadence typical of the people up here. I resist trying to fill the gaps with my words.

"The water... It's no place to be in wind like this."

Billy must be in his mid- to late seventies and is showing his age. He looks and acts much older than Eileen. He's heavy-set and his pants are held up high with bright red suspenders. A black Buffalo Airways ball cap sits high on his brow.

"We shouldn't have this wind blowing from there, where it's blowing now, from the northeast," he says. "Our bad winds come from the northwest."

"Have you seen any other big changes over the years, Billy?" I ask.

"Last couple years we really have to watch the ice while traveling. It doesn't freeze as well as it used to do. You have to be careful in the fall traveling with your snow machine."

Billy and Eileen have a hunting cabin at tree line, to the south, and spend much of the year there.

"We have magpies in the last three years at the cabin, shouldn't be there. Lots of tree squirrels now. They're everywhere now."

Billy speaks of polar bears being stranded onshore because of the lack of ice, and even of signs of them at his cabin.

"Even inside our tree line there's been polar bear tracks."

Several hours go by in easy banter, and we reluctantly bid farewell to our friendly hosts, knowing we need to make final preparations before heading out. Tuktoyaktuk is the last community we'll be in for some time, so it's now or never for purchasing anything extra we want. The wind is forecast to subside by midnight tonight, and we intend to head out as soon as it does. We hope the storm has broken up the ice off the Tuk Peninsula and that travel will now be easier, but we have no idea what really awaits us.

5

DRAGGING ON
THE TUKTOYAKTUK
PENINSULA

"FRANK, CHECK IT OUT!!" I scream, pointing to the rear of the boat. "Over there, in the surf." The porcelain white head easily breaches the water, the bemused expression and bulbous forehead unmistakable: a beluga whale. "Look, it's staring at us."

Our surprise at seeing it is likely matched by its surprise at seeing us, two guys dragging a boat through surf. It's an altogether different world here, but it's in moments like this, when a beluga whale surfaces a mere twenty yards away, that this really hits home.

The prevailing winds through this section of the Northwest Passage are northwesterlies, but this season they've come only from the east and northeast. As Billy Jacobsen pointed out, it's been a strange year so far, and the anomalous winds are making for tough going not only for the beluga hunters, but for us as well.

"He's having an easier time than us," I lament as the white head disappears. "For now, anyhow," I mumble to myself as I realize what might await him farther west at the Mackenzie Delta hunting ground.

We've managed to row nonstop for the last twenty hours since leaving Tuktoyaktuk, riding calm seas and tidal currents to our advantage, but things have changed. It's 2:30 a.m. on Monday, July 15, and the dreaded northeasterlies have returned. "We came to row the Northwest Passage, not walk it," I say to Frank, trying to be upbeat, but not sure I'm succeeding.

"At least we're moving forward," he responds with feigned enthusiasm.

Manhandling a boat the size of the *Arctic Joule* is similar to pushing a car—the more severe the resistance, the slower you push—and the force of the wind equates to the incline of a road. Wave action plays into the equation, with the ocean swell hitting the boat broadside, rocking her wildly and pushing her on top of us. On this section of the Tuktoyaktuk Peninsula, the frigid ocean water of the Beaufort Sea mixes with the outflow of the warmer Mackenzie River, resulting in a temperature that, by Arctic standards, is warm. That's good news for us at the moment, as we're submerged waist deep, waves lapping around us as we push, and we're drenched.

We're kitted for the worst, though. Our inner layers consist of heavy wool socks on the feet and a combination of underwear and fleece on both top and bottom. The underwear wicks the moisture away from the skin, and fleece provides insulation. Over this we've slipped ourselves into arguably our most important piece of clothing—our burly one-piece dry suits. "They're the absolute bomb," Frank said enthusiastically when he first secured sponsorship from the manufacturer, Ocean Rodeo. "It's a new design with a fully integrated VENTOR sock system. There's nothing better out there. We'll stay bone dry." Over the integrated socks, neoprene booties, and gloves protect our feet and hands. We're wearing it all now, even in this relatively warm water.

We remain in the water a lot over the next couple days. We row when we can but find ourselves pushing more than anything. It's disheartening work more conducive to disassociation than banter, and I find we're all listening to our iPods more and more. Music helps the mind drift.

"Whatch'ya listening to?" I yell to Frank, trying to out-volume the sound from his iPod, the wind, and the waves. He's pushing at the bow of the boat, directing the nose through the rolling surf; I'm pushing at the stern. "Keef," he replies, imitating an East London accent. "Johnny Depp's reading now." He's listening to the audiobook of Keith Richard's autobiography. I'm next in line, but for now I have Pink Floyd on deck, a perfect psychedelic mix for the heavenly show onstage.

The landscape here is so low-lying that the sky is the only scenic canvas. This evening's display is an arcing sweep of white cotton-ball dabs on a baby blue background. Strokes of light, seemingly etched from a celestial brush, sweep radially across the canvas, their source of brilliance somewhere beyond the frame.

We manage several shifts of pushing but we're forced to stop by deteriorating conditions. When a small sandy inlet conveniently appears, we tuck ourselves into the lee of a sandbank and wait for things to improve. Denis is cleaning one of the shotguns on deck and I'm standing opposite him, my backside resting against the spare oars that act as our safety rail on deck.

"I wonder if we'll see a bear anytime soon," Denis says. "We'll see it coming, anyhow," he adds, nodding toward the flat, sandy landscape. The scene before us could easily be mistaken for the Caribbean, with its clear blue skies, white sandy beaches, and aquamarine water. Only the cold wind sets an Arctic tone.

"It's the bear we *don't* see coming that I'm worried about," I say. "I'm happy we have this sturdy cabin to sleep in."

Back in 1993, two Vancouver kayakers traveled these waters attempting to traverse a section of the Northwest Passage. They were camped very close to where we are now, sleeping through the wee hours of the morning, when a powerful blow came through the tent wall, knocking adventurer Phil Torrens from his back to his stomach. He felt a searing pain in his shoulder as something penetrated it, then the terrifying sensation of teeth tearing into his scalp. He surmises that his screams for help made the attacker stop. His shotgun had been beside him when he slept but was now under the crumpled fabric of the flattened tent. He groped for it, kicking and punching wildly at the fabric, and found it just in time to be attacked again. Torrens passed the gun to his teammate as his assailant latched onto his leg and began rag-dolling him around the tent. Torrens's tentmate put the shotgun to his shoulder and took blind aim but hesitated when he realized that an injured polar bear would likely be even more dangerous than a hungry one. He aimed upward instead, fired one round, and the attack ended.[1] Although Torrens survived the mauling, the pair required an immediate rescue and their expedition came to an abrupt end. We all knew this story well coming into this expedition, and it surfaces among us from time to time.

"What would we do if we all woke to a polar bear on deck?" I ask, throwing the question out more in jest than anything else. "I'd give it a blast of the air horn," Denis says, and Paul, listening to us from the cabin, quickly gives us an unexpected demonstration. The piercing blast or the marine horn makes us jump. "Jesus Christ!" I scream. "That scared the shit out of me!"

We keep a shotgun in the cabin at all times, tucked into the fabric of the wall-mounted mesh, and we keep a keen eye on its cleanliness. Shotguns can jam if not kept clean and oiled—not something we wish to deal with in a polar bear encounter.

IN RECENT DAYS, Paul and Denis have been recording a three-minute daily video diary on Paul's iPhone about the trials and tribulations of the journey. They typically shoot it when Frank and I are on the oars and out of earshot but show it to us at the end of the day.

"We like doing these video diaries," Denis says, laughing, "because we watch them back ten minutes later and it's like watching TV with yourself on it."

"And we think we're both hilarious," Paul says.

The video posts can vary from a serious discussion of the day's events to a poking match between the two. Regardless, they're always entertaining.

VIDEO DIARY, DAY 14

DENIS: In the Big Brother house, and I just had to watch Paul relieve himself off the back of the boat.

PAUL: Over the last twenty-four hours we haven't gone that far. We're only doing two and a half kilometers per hour.

DENIS: And we're at the mercy of the wind.

PAUL: Yeah, we're at the mercy of Denis's wind.

It hasn't taken long for all of us to fall into specific roles on this expedition, and one I've fallen into is communications. I became familiar with the challenges of satellite communications when I traveled to the South Pole in 2008–9, and I bring that experience to our expedition now. All our data communication needs for the trip are pushed through an Iridium 9505a satellite phone, which can only handle data at a rate of 14 kilobytes per minute. To put this in perspective, the Nikon D600 I'm shooting with is storing images at roughly 25 megabytes (25,000 kilobytes) per image. Sending one image at that size would take nearly 29.76 hours of satellite time. With satellite rates running about $2.50 a minute, and assuming we had the battery power and patience to do it, it would cost us $4,464 to send that one image. We accommodate sending some by keeping files tiny, and the satellite phone automatically rejects any incoming messages that exceed 50 kilobytes. Our setup is working well, and the essential information—weather and ice data—is getting through.

In addition to the daily ice and weather reports from the Canadian Ice Service, we receive routine emails from a weather router who's helping us out. A few months before our departure, we received an email from a man named Victor offering to help us with route-finding as we move through the Passage. Although Victor apparently traveled the Northwest

Passage at some point and seems to know our route well, he's enigmatic—going only by his first name, keeping his location secret, and generally remaining in the shadows. His writing style suggests Russian descent, though we have no way of knowing. He's not charging us for his services, but to date he seems extremely thorough. On one of my routine communication checks, I receive an alarming email from him. The message is unequivocal: "Unwise to move ahead, you are ready for your route but your route is not ready for you."

We're still in the lee of our sandbank. The wind is pumping and we've gone nowhere. I stick my head out of the cabin and yell to the guys on deck: "You boys should come in here and read this. I got a strange email from Victor." The message continues at length, indicating that pack ice sits not far offshore, these northerly winds could push it down on us, and we should consider turning around, heading back to Tuk, and waiting until things improve. By the end of the message, it dawns on us that Victor sees the *Arctic Joule* more as a swift-moving sailboat than the sluggish behemoth it is. His email suggests that we can make huge mileage when the ice shifts, but ice is not our enemy at the moment: wind is. He doesn't fully comprehend that clawing forward, no matter how slowly, is our only hope of making this crossing. We have no choice but to maintain forward movement, albeit with heightened caution. We will move as close to the ice edge as possible and be ready to jump when it breaks.

As we muse over our dilemma, an icy fog replaces the sun, leaving us with nothing to do but wait. Sunday brings high cloud, lighter winds, and a renewed sense of vigor. We'll move forward, keeping a sharp eye out for ice.

We move up the coast and for the first time begin to see ice floes on the seascape. Initially, they look like oddly shaped profiles on the horizon, elongated and stretched, seeming far bigger than they actually are. This is an interesting phenomenon in the Arctic: objects on the horizon appear to be stretched vertically as if manipulated by a lens to peer over the visual plane. Islands can look much bigger than they are and at times seem to float above the horizon, like dark blobs suspended in space.

The ice first comes in small pans no bigger than thirty square feet, but over the course of the day they become more frequent and varied in size. With the ice comes an Arctic fog that creates an otherworldly feel. It obscures our view, and we row into one partially submerged chunk of ice the size of a dinner table, which gives us a heart-skipping thump.

Frank and I are asleep and in the cabin when we round Point Atkinson and start traversing McKinley Bay. It's the morning of Wednesday, July 17, and the weather has turned calm and warm. I poke my head out of the cabin, barely believing what I see.

"It's beautiful out!"

"Yeah, about an hour after you guys went down, *this* happened," Denis says, grinning.

I think back to just three hours ago, when we finished our shift.

"The sun must have burned off the fog," I say. "It scared off the ice too, it seems."

We make our crossing in a rare moment of tranquility, the sea smooth and reflective as a mirror.

From space, the Tuktoyaktuk Peninsula loosely resembles a human finger pointing northeast from its base at the village of Tuktoyaktuk to its tip at Cape Dalhousie, where it bends due north after the final knuckle in Russell Inlet. McKinley Bay is located at the middle knuckle, and connecting it with Russell Inlet and the cape is a large lobe of land that, from miles above the earth, looks like an arcing chunk of Swiss cheese, but with more holes. The holes are lakes, but they're inland and don't affect us. The fragmented coastline, nibbled and gnawed on, is a different matter. We made it across McKinley Bay and are now rounding the lobe. Our sandy coast has been replaced by a disjointed array of islets, isthmuses, sandbars, and shoals.

On one occasion, Frank and I push out into deeper water in search of the elusive east-moving current that's supposed to be out there. We're exposed to the full brunt of a twenty-knot headwind mixed with a negative tidal current and are literally pushed backward.

"Christ, this is nuts," I say. "I don't think we're moving at all!"

"Yeah, we're moving all right," Frank says after looking at his GPS. "We're moving backward. We gotta get out of this."

We attempt to ferry back to shore only to become grounded on a series of sandbars hiding beneath the surface. The water is only knee deep, yet we're stranded miles offshore in the middle of the Arctic Ocean. We both jump from the boat and start pushing, but it's no use.

"Paul, Denis, we need help out here," I yell to the boys inside. "We're really stuck this time."

Being at the mercy of the wind like this is both confounding and discomfiting, and reinforces our awareness of the *Arctic Joule*'s limitations.

There's no question that a smaller vessel like a kayak would perform better in such wind and shallow water. The smaller size would mean less windage and a reduced draft, which was undoubtedly why the ancestors of today's local Indigenous population developed it. But for our purposes, it would also mean less carrying capacity and reduced seaworthiness. We struggled with this balance in the design of the *Arctic Joule* and at one point even contemplated building a smaller, non-self-righting vessel. We could have made the hull out of a lighter, less ice-resistant material, left the 145-pound safety raft behind, and done a number of things to lighten her up, but we didn't. Instead we decided to build a resilient vessel that would always be up to the task of traversing these unforgiving waters. Approaching an expedition like ours with a devil-may-care attitude would expose not only the participants to undue risk, but also any rescuers who would be called in if something went wrong. The participants have a choice; their rescuers don't.

We didn't take that approach. *The Arctic Joule* is a strong, seaworthy vessel that performs excellently under certain conditions and not so well under others. We've understood this all along and need to bear with it now when she's under strain. We manage to push her off the sandbar with considerable effort and head into the lee of a nearby island to wait out the wind.

WHEN A CULTURE and a people have a specific word to describe a specific action, you know that action bears heavily on their life. To the Inuit *quinuituq* means "deep patience." Southerners have no such word.

For a vessel under sail or motor, the winds hampering us now would be of little consequence. But strong easterlies and northeasterlies stymie our human-powered rowboat, claw at our speed, gnaw at our souls. If I think back to the toughest moments of past expeditions, they always seem to have revolved around a forced holdup: being tent-bound in a windstorm a stone's throw from the South Pole and running out of food as we ran out of time; being stormbound on the edge of the frozen Bering Sea and having to cross it to complete the expedition but knowing it would break up soon; being stranded by floods while traversing South America, almost finished the expedition but with no route through. All these episodes were frustrating because they were all beyond my control.

The Arctic takes the concept of the forced wait to another level, as described in some of the reading material we've brought along. Three books doing the rounds in the cabin are Pierre Berton's tome *The Arctic Grail: The Quest for the North West Passage and the North Pole 1818–1909,* Bruce Macdonald's *North Star of Herschel Island,* and Barry Lopez's modern masterpiece of Arctic observation, *Arctic Dreams.* Lopez sums up the common thread running through all of these books when he states simply that "to travel in the Arctic is to wait." Long episodes of waiting have defined every historical expedition through the Northwest Passage—waiting for weather, waiting for ice, waiting for the passage to let them through. Our expedition is no different. And so we wait.

EVERY EVENING FRANK takes the time to smoke a single Indonesian clove cigarette. He developed a taste for them on our 2001 volcano-climbing expedition in Java and brings them on all his expeditions now. It's odd seeing such a high-level athlete—he's without a doubt one of the best all-around athletes I've ever met—puffing away on a cigarette, but that dichotomy is all Frank. Tonight he dons a blood red robe much like a Japanese kimono that he's brought on the trip for exactly these occasions, and sits alone at the bow rowing station facing back at the rear cabin. He's pulled a white and green Molson Export beer toque down over his ears, he's holding his clove cigarette in one hand and a stainless-steel flask of whiskey in the other, and a loaded shotgun lies across his lap.

We stare out at him through the plexiglass of the cabin hatch as he puffs and sips. "They haven't locked them all up yet," Denis says, laughing. "He's an odd duck, that Frank."

IT'S NIGHTTIME ON Wednesday, July 18, and we've traveled just a little over seventy miles since leaving Tuk five days ago. We expected to average a minimum of thirty miles per day and secretly hoped for a lot more. We never anticipated this.

VIDEO DIARY, DAY 15

DENIS: We've only come two hundred kilometers in two fucking weeks. We had a talk today about if we're going to run out of food before we get to the fucking halfway point. If it stays this way for the next two months we'll only cover 20 percent of our objective—it's that fucked up. Pond Inlet may as well be on the fucking moon.

PAUL: With our boat, it's just fucking not happening. (*He shakes his head.*) The old fellas [Frank and I] are dragging the boat now.

DENIS: Every island is joined to another island by a sandbar. We're dragging the boat like a big fucking horse.

PAUL: There's a bar in Dublin called the Sand Bar. (*He laughs.*) I can never go into a bar called fucking Sand Bar ever again.

Like the boys, I'm prone to swearing when I'm mad. My father was too. He told me that on O'Connell Street in Dublin he once saw a man, walking along, who saw a laborer slip and fall off a ladder in front of a bus. The man screamed out, "Fuck! The fucker's fucking fucked!" It's an Irish thing, evidently.

THE WINDS REMAIN unabated through the overnight hours. Frank stays awake and slips out of the cabin periodically to see if there's a change. By five in the morning, things begin to ease.

"I think we should give it a shot," Frank says, waking me from my slumber. "The wind seems to be dying a bit."

I've been asleep only a few hours and find it difficult to get going.

"Sounds good," I mumble, lying.

Waking up like this is always hard for me, but not for Frank: he never sleeps. Frank is easily one of the toughest individuals I know, never displaying weakness in any difficult situation. The one chink in his armor is that he's an incredibly light sleeper. Even the slightest noise will rouse him, and once he's awake, he's up for the day. On the several expeditions I've done with him, he's typically last to bed and first to rise. He shrugs it off as the reality of adventure.

"I don't sleep much on trips," he tells people. "It doesn't affect me."

So staying awake and checking conditions often falls to Frank. The conditions have improved and we decide to get moving. Our small islet is fully exposed to the wind, leaving us few options. We must move toward the mainland. For the *Arctic Joule,* strong winds in open water mean being pushed backward or holding fast at anchor. Strong winds close to shore give us choices: we can use island lees and peninsulas to hide and maneuver behind, and beaches to drag the boat when rowing is impossible. This is our strategy and it's working, albeit slowly.

Frank and I ferry from our island perch to a series of smaller islets, which provide a semblance of protection from the ever-present wind. The crossing is exhilarating, with fast, dark rollers sweeping beneath our bow, their tips frothing, their valleys deep.

It's a glorious morning. A wash of radiant ocher bathes everything in an animated glow. We spy two large caribou staring intently at us from a small island, antlers soaring and provocative, their stance exuding astonishment. We see countless more caribou over the course of the day, a forest of antlers often the only hint of the animals in repose.

Our easterly wind shifts to northeasterly and we begin to make some guarded progress at the oars. We cross two large, heaving bays of rollers and pull back a little lost mileage. The movement buoys our spirits.

When conditions permit, we move twenty-four hours a day—each team rowing or pushing for three hours and resting for three hours, until the weather stops us—which makes it difficult to discern one day from the next. Evenings are a little colder and darker than midday, but the ambient daylight even in the middle of the night is adequate to read by. The sun never sets. It took some getting used to, but after living it for the past couple of weeks, it's becoming a routine.

We round Cape Dalhousie at the tip of the Tuktoyaktuk Peninsula on Wednesday, July 24, eleven days after leaving Tuk. For days, we've been looking forward to the moment when we'd finally feel a little wind at our stern heading south into Liverpool Bay. Murphy was an Irishman, I suppose, and must be taking a keen interest in our expedition because the wind shifts to east-northeast as we make the turn. Although forecasted to weaken, it rapidly builds into a stormy blow. We hold firm, convinced it will subside, and keep pushing down the coast. Instead, the waves grow larger and steeper until we're negotiating the biggest seas we've seen on the expedition. The water at Cape Dalhousie is exceedingly shallow, and big rollers are becoming dangerous breakers all around us. Sandbars pop up seemingly out of nowhere, every one representing a potential shipwreck in this turbulent seascape.

Within an hour we start looking for an exit strategy and realize we may have left this discussion longer than we should have. There was a way out on the coast, but it has become barred by a continuous sandbar running parallel with the shore. A calm body of water lies tantalizingly close on the other side, impossible to reach. Trying to negotiate the surf zone would be catastrophic for the *Arctic Joule,* and us.

Paul and Denis finish their shift and Frank and I take over. It's a tenuous shift change: the potential of a wave swamping the boat is always a risk when crew members are moving in and out of the cabin. I stand behind Paul at his rowing station as he gets up with a groan. "Arggh, there you go, Kev." Paul's bum hip is stiff after his shift. I replace him in the rowing seat while Denis keeps rowing to hold the boat on the correct angle to the waves. As I start to row, Frank and Denis change places. A moment's inattention could see the boat swing broadside to the waves.

In all my expeditions, I've never been in seas this large, and I feel both anxiety and exhilaration. Steep walls of black water build out of nothing and run at us, tips frothing. But no sooner are they upon us than they're sweeping under our bow on a steady trajectory to an explosive end onshore. We're not their target yet, but we keep a close eye on them to ensure that doesn't change.

After ninety tense minutes of rowing, a break in the sandbar appears and we decide to go for it, turning the boat in to shore and running with the waves. This is the most dangerous position to be in, because a large wave can surf the boat, swiftly turn her broadside, and roll her. My heart's in my mouth as a large wave builds behind us, rolls up on our stern, and pushes us aggressively.

The Arctic Joule is a big gal. Her weight and girth are a challenge in headwinds and over sandbars, but she's in her element here. The wave doesn't push her around; she holds her course, comfortable in these waters. My oar catches on one wave and bends horribly but doesn't break. A few more tenuous minutes and we're in calmer waters.

"We're in the game now," Paul says as Frank and I enter the cabin.

Paul has webbing strung from the roof of the cabin and he's stretching his hip. Denis sits across from him, resting against his sleeping bag.

"Fancy a cup of tea, lads?"

We strip out of our dry suits and start our forced layover.

"A bar o' *chocolat*?" Paul asks, opening a bar, breaking it into pieces, and laying it out on the wrapper at our feet. We're used to this ritual now—tea and chocolate in hand, killing time any way we can. Today Frank and Denis have locked into Denis's iPod and take turns playing a Tiger Woods golf game while Paul and I scribble away in our journals.

With all four of us crammed into the small cabin and the hatches closed due to the storm, condensation builds quickly.

It's not long before water is beading on every edge above us and starts dripping, making everything damp.

"I'm shag tired," Paul says, resting his journal on his lap and laying his head back.

"Yeah, you get a bit tired, I suppose . . . and wet," Denis says. I sense he's not done. "But, em, Paul is still managing to keep up a furious masturbation schedule at the same time, which is phenomenal. No one else is even thinking about it, but he's beating away. I've been calling him Jack instead of Paul."

I'm enjoying the lighthearted ribbing between these two. Denis typically comes out on top with his quick wit. I never know what he's going to say next. He fell off the boat yesterday at a point when we transitioned from pushing to rowing. The sandbar had given away to deeper water and he wasn't ready for it. His dry suit, unzipped and open at the neck, filled with icy seawater. He clambered back on board quickly enough, but I could see embarrassment in his face. His video diary confirmed this. "Became the first swimmer of the expedition today. I slipped off the boat. I had my dry suit on but it was unzipped. The water was very cold. Lesson learned. Not great . . . I'd say the lads aren't too impressed."

OUR LAYOVER IN the sandbar lee is short as we're eager to make our first big open-water crossing from Liverpool Bay to Cape Bathurst Peninsula. If we had our choice we'd have made a number of larger crossings already, but conditions have made this impossible.

We begin rowing across Liverpool Bay in the early hours of the evening. Winds are predicted to dissipate by midnight and our hope is that the seas will diminish as well. But the moment we pull out from the sandbar lee, we are hit with a jolt. The waves are sharper and tighter in rhythm than before. A strong sense of ill ease washes over me, but Frank and I are committed to our line and we keep our tempo high.

The boat rocks wildly, and for the first time this trip a strong sensation of nausea starts to well up in my gut. I put it out of my mind and focus on watching for the next wave, trying to time my oar stroke to catch it and trying not to hit Frank's oars in the process.

The steep faces of water that bear down on us have such a menacing presence that I start to focus on them only after they've rolled up under the boat and are charging away from us. My ostrich approach to disquiet begins to work for me.

Our plan is to make a direct line across to Cape Wolki— I can only assume it's named for the Wolki family of which Jim and Fred are members, but I'm not certain—on the Cape Bathurst Peninsula, but the strong north wind does not subside as forecast and we're driven farther south to Nicholson Island, home to another Cold War–era DEW Line radar station, about two-thirds of the way across the bay.

Frank and I put in our three-hour shift and hand things over to the boys. The rough seas keep us awake, and before we know it we're up again for our next stint. We see Nicholson Island poking over the heaving horizon but it never seems to get any closer; we're still only halfway across Liverpool Bay. The next three hours proves an exhausting test of will and tenacity as the seas stay huge, and so do our efforts. We know that if the wind builds any more, we might be blown completely off course. By the end of our shift we slip into the cabin, wanting only sleep.

"How about we eat and drink after a quick nap?" I ask Frank.

"Yeah, sounds good," he says, already out of his dry suit and into his sleeping bag.

"I'll set the alarm for 6:00 a.m.," I say.

It's just after 4:00 a.m. now, and that will allow us an hour to eat, drink, and get ready before heading out again. The rocking of the boat gently subsides and I fall asleep immediately.

"LAND HO!" PAUL yells. I'm startled awake, heart pounding, and sit straight up in my sleeping bag.

"What?" I mumble as I peer out the porthole window to see steep grassland rising from a sandy beach. "We're across!"

6

NEAR DISASTER
ON FRANKLIN BAY

NICHOLSON ISLAND COULDN'T HAVE APPEARED at a better moment. The northerly wind we've been fighting has pushed us deep into Liverpool Bay; if it weren't for the island, we'd be at the bottom of the bay now. Paul and Denis row us in close to shore and toss the anchor. We're about fifty yards out, the water is only a couple of feet deep, and we easily walk in. The DEW Line station we spied on our crossing sits at the high point of the island several miles away. We all shuffle to shore and slip out of our dry suits.

"We fucking stink," Denis says, tossing his dry suit over a log. "Christ, my socks smell."

"Yeah, Denear, I can smell you from here," Paul says.

We're only on the beach for a few minutes when a large arctic fox lumbers over the rise and strides directly toward us. Its hair is ragged, a dirty mix of red and white, and it dances along nonplussed by our arrival. It gets within one hundred feet of us before it stops, apparently catching our scent, and scampers off into the brush. The mosquitos aren't as easily swayed by our odor and find us by the thousands. Although our clothes and hats protect us from the bulk of their attacks, such waves of them sweep over us that it becomes difficult to do much but swat them. A pair of hawks have discovered us as well and screech overhead, agitated and aggressive, likely guarding a nearby nest.

Our stretch of beach, at the northern end of Nicholson Island, extends eastward from the body of the island like a tendril, pushing out into Liverpool Bay for well over half a mile and getting ever narrower until it sweeps into an arc at its end. We scamper over its backbone to a small bay with a sandy beach running south. An eroding bank of mud and rock hems the beach, giving way to rolling fields of brownish-green tundra that bump along ever upward to the DEW Line station. The surface of the sand we're walking along is an indented tapestry of hoofprints, and I begin to ask the obvious question when it's answered for me.

"There they are!" Denis shouts as a herd of caribou rumble down a small gully to the beach just ahead of us. "Uh, guys, they're coming this way. Maybe we should let them by?" The caribou are skittish and move toward us in fits and starts, clearly wanting to pass us but apprehensive to do so. They're agitated and quiver uncontrollably, shaking their heads back and forth, apparently driven as mad by the mosquitos as we are. We move to the side and crouch down, but the big bull at the front remains uncertain, charging up the steep slope adjacent to us and galloping past with the herd following behind.

They move like a flock of birds, the animals in the back following the leader's every move, as they race past us in wild-eyed abandon.

These animals are barren-ground caribou, likely from the Cape Bathurst herd, but they may have a little reindeer blood in them as well. Reindeer aren't native to this region, but back in the late 1920s they were brought into the Mackenzie Delta because of dwindling caribou numbers. The decline in caribou was so significant at the time that the local Inuvialuit, who depended heavily on caribou for food, began to starve. The Canadian government, recognizing the emergency, purchased some three thousand reindeer from a company in western Alaska and hired Sami herders from northern Europe to drive them east across the breadth of Alaska and northern Yukon to the Mackenzie Delta. The initiative helped the starving people of the region in the short term but never really took off in the long term as caribou numbers rebounded. The reindeer herd was eventually moved inland, but not before introducing reindeer genetics into the indigenous caribou herds. Today it's not known how many animals around the Tuktoyaktuk Peninsula are feral reindeer or caribou–reindeer hybrids.

The cyclical nature of caribou numbers is interesting and not fully understood. Over the last couple of decades, barren-ground caribou numbers have gone into steep decline again. The Cape Bathurst herd decreased from 19,300 animals in the 1990s to a mere 2,400 in 2012,[1] the Bathurst population dropped by about a third after 2012, and the Tuktoyaktuk Peninsula population dropped to only 1,701 animals, a decline of 500 since 2012. But some Inuvialuit people suggest the dramatic changes may not be cause for alarm.

"Caribou has a fifty- to seventy-year cycle of coming and going," the deputy mayor of Tuktoyaktuk, Darrel Nasogaluak, said when we spoke to him a couple of weeks back. "Traditional knowledge says it's cyclical. We didn't have caribou back here until the late seventies and early eighties." He suggested that the herds swell and shrink and move to different regions over the years in a pattern that's very familiar to his people. His traditional knowledge suggests not to be overly concerned by the drop, but he's conscious of new outside factors as well.

"When a herd goes from 460,000 to 15,000, to me and I think everybody else, that's an emergency," says Michael Miltenberger, the Northwest Territories' Minister of Environment and Natural Resources, referring to the Bathurst herd's population in 1986 and now. Scientists believe climate change is also playing a role in the decline as seasonal temperatures shift and industrial development creeps farther north, but what role is not yet fully understood.

"Although the evidence is incomplete, we suspect these further declines, in large part, reflect poor environmental conditions, possibly on the summer range, [which] are leading to reduced pregnancy rates and reduced calf survival rates," says Jan Adamczewski, a wildlife biologist with the territory's Department of Environment and Natural Resources.

The territorial government says the problem is not unique to the Northwest Territories, either: Alaska and Nunavut are experiencing similar declines. "The longer term issue," Miltenberger says, "is to come up with a management plan and to get the players to the table and finally develop a Bathurst management plan that everybody will agree with." [2]

I watch the caribou race over the spine of the peninsula we just crossed and charge down to its far end. "Where the hell are they running to?" I ask. "It's a dead end down there. Obviously not the brightest of creatures."

We poke around a bit more and head back to the boat. We've been gone only an hour but the tide's already out. *The Arctic Joule* is beached on the sand and we're stuck here until the next high tide. The wind has died as well. It would seem the caribou aren't the only dumb animals on this beach.

The mosquitos have become suffocating in the calm air. "Hey, check out the caribou now," I say, pointing to the end of the slender spit. "They're all out in the water." The caribou were fixated on passing us because they were trying to get into the sea. The entire herd is now neck deep in water, standing motionless, enjoying a little respite from the mosquitos, leaving the real dummies staring at them, and at their boat, from the land.

Frank pulls out a clove cigarette and his flask of whiskey. "If we can't row," he says, raising them high with a grin, "we might as well enjoy." I'm not a smoker, but I love the aroma of clove tobacco. I was first introduced to it at the same time as Frank, back in Java. The adventure went sideways from the start. We arrived in Jakarta on my birthday, the day before 9/11. Over the next three weeks, the world changed around us and we soon became lone Westerners traveling through the largest Muslim country in the world in the midst of a jihad. We finally fled the country after being threatened on several occasions and scoped by a man with a rifle. The experience didn't sully my love of Indonesia and its people, though—I've been back since—and the smell of clove tobacco always brings me back to that exotic land.

"Just hold the smoke in your mouth when you sip the single malt," Frank says as I give it a try. "It gives a peaty taste."

Frank is filming our journey for us and is quick to pull out the camera. "Kevin, what are we looking at here?"

"DEW Line station thataway," I say, pointing up the hill. "Herd of caribou thataway," I say, pointing to the end of the spit. "We literally had a herd of caribou run right by us a couple minutes ago."

"Yeah, yeah. Paul was running after one with what looked like a lipstick hanging out of his pants," Denis adds.

Resigned to the forced break, we set about cleaning up the boat and drying out gear, and the boys even swim in the icy waters as I take a catnap in the cabin. But the metallic castle on the hill beckons, and after doing everything we can at the boat, we load up with cameras and a shotgun and head toward it.

We walk toward two large metal storage containers high on the bank above the shore about half a mile distant. We spotted them earlier, but the caribou herd threw us off. The gray structures are the size of rectangular one-story garages and sit close beside one another. Fuel pipes lead from each and merge into a central line that runs to the edge of the eroded slope facing the beach. Warning signs painted on the container scream, "DANGER. No Smoking within 50 feet."

We can see a faint roadway in the tundra leading inland from the containers in the direction of a gently sloping ridge that rises to the DEW Line station. We follow the road for a short time but break from it the moment it meanders. The tundra is inviting for a walker, but its hummocky surface is uneven and soft. I'm cautious not to twist an ankle. It takes us an hour of steady trekking before we crest the final rise and see the Distant Early Warning radar station in all its glory, a strange conglomeration of industrial architecture as natural in this landscape as a polar bear in the Sahara.

A blue, rectangular, metal-clad building, roughly fifteen feet high, forty feet wide, and one hundred feet long, occupies the center of the grouping of structures. An open metal walkway, wide enough to accommodate a large vehicle, rises gently from the tundra up to a double-sized entry door on the building's facade. There's a distinct diesel smell coming from the building. For some unknown reason, the building itself seems to be chugging; though it's likely that some machinery is operating inside it, the oddness of it adds to our sense of disquiet. Two white geodesic domes, each about forty feet in diameter and resembling giant golf balls, sit at the far end of the blue building. Another white dome of the same size sits high above everything on a seven-story tower. Four gray fuel-storage boxes, identical to the two we investigated by the water, sit neatly aligned adjacent to the tower. All the structures rest on metal pylons, where they almost appear to be suspended a full story above the tundra.

These radar stations, designed and built in the late 1950s, during the Cold War, were the primary line of air defense for detecting Russian incursions into North American airspace. The DEW Line initiative consisted of a string of sixty-three radar and communication centers stretching from western Alaska across the Canadian Arctic to Greenland. By the early 1990s, most of the stations had been deactivated, with only a few left operational. This radar station now operates as an unattended short-range radar station, part of the new North Warning System, which provides airspace surveillance to warn of potential incursions across North America's polar region.

There's something strangely foreboding about the steady grind of a motor washing over stark industrial structures with no trace of a human presence. The station would fit seamlessly into a child's imagining of what a Martian space station might look like—bleak, austere, and vaguely military. The whole place makes me uneasy.

The site is home to a small herd of caribou, which are currently huddled under one of the white radar domes. It's windier up here than below, but not windy enough to keep the mosquitos at bay. The animals look as agitated as their friends on the beach and begin moving again as soon as the wind eases. They don't appear scared of us, and a few seem completely oblivious.

The animals are ragged; the fuzz of their white winter coat is giving way to the fine dark brown hair of their summer skin. They run around us in a flurry, stopping for a moment to graze until a shudder seems to radiate through their bodies, leaving their skin trembling and heads shaking, and they begin to move again, the mosquitos their constant foe. Some members of the herd boast enormous antlers that rise over three feet above their heads, like small leafless trees covered in beige velvet.

We walk up the metal gangway to the oversized door of the main building. "Maybe we can go inside," Denis says, but a sign by the door says otherwise: "Government Property. No Trespassing. This site is monitored by remote video camera." We sneak a peek in the main door only to see that it's a vestibule, with double doors on the opposite wall saying "Keep Out." There's an old push-button phone on the wall. Suddenly a voice booms from a loudspeaker outside the building: "Personnel on site please call base. Call NTF at 3500."

"Are they talking to us?" Denis asks. The message roars out of the speakers again. Denis steps over to the phone and picks it up. "I'll see what they want—3500, right?" After a short pause he begins talking. I can barely hear his voice over the rumble of motors within the building. All I catch at the end of the conversation is "Okay, okay, we'll leave."

As he hangs up, Frank asks, "What did they say?"

"We don't have approval to be here. We can't go in and have a look around. He didn't seem too pushed, though. Not much he can do about it anyhow," he says, laughing. "He's probably two thousand miles away."

I'm happy to head back to the boat; this robo-station is giving me the creeps, and a hawk screeching above us is reinforcing that feeling. By the time we get back to the *Arctic Joule,* the tide is beginning to creep back and it's not long before we're afloat again.

"I'm happy to get away from this missile fucking defense system as quickly as we can," Denis says as we push off. "Don't like the feel of this place."

We bid farewell to Nicholson Island on calm seas and head east to the Bathurst Peninsula. It's a pleasant change from the rough conditions of previous days, with seas like glass and temperatures in the mid-twenties. We row continuously for the next twenty-six hours on smooth waters and positive currents, swing up past Cape Wolki, and head north to the tip of Cape Bathurst. Before leaving on the expedition, I met with Dr. Bill Williams from the Department of Fisheries and Oceans in Sidney, British Columbia. He warned me of very swift wind-driven currents sweeping around the tip of Cape Bathurst at speeds high enough to stop us in our tracks. We approach the tip of the peninsula with trepidation.

As we round Cape Bathurst, the wind begins to build. It's subtle at first, a light riffle across an otherwise glassy surface, but it grows quickly in force. The cape presents a vertical black wall of permafrost, which rises some fifty feet from water's edge. A green carpet of tundra bends and tumbles from atop, its upper surface pulled seaward by the eroding bank. It's an imposing sight—a sheer icy wall extending into the mist, making retreat impossible if things turn bad. And they do.

The wind intensifies sharply, pushing us directly toward the cliffs. The water here is shallow and, as the seas build, so does the steepness of the waves. Soon whitecaps are everywhere. By the time we reach the most exposed section of the cape, the sea is in a frenzy. Waves find the shallow spots in the undulating shoals below and explode around us, washing over the deck. I'm watching all this from the confines of the cabin. The boys are still in their fleece from the nice rowing a couple of hours ago. The storm hit us so quickly they had no time to get into their dry suits. A fall overboard now would be catastrophic. Submersion in the icy water without a dry suit would mean almost immediate incapacitation, and a rescue would be very difficult.

As it stands, it's taking all hands just to keep us off the cliffs. The boat is bucking like an angry bull and we can't allow her to sweep broadside to the waves this close to shore. It's Frank's and my turn at the oars, and we make our seat changes one at a time, as quickly as we can. I replace Paul at the bow seat while Denis continues to row, fighting solo to keep us facing into the waves. When I start rowing, Frank replaces Denis.

We need to find shelter from the storm, but we won't find it under those cliffs. We turn the *Arctic Joule* out to sea and start fighting. The waves and wind are pushing hard but we keep the bow pointed at forty-five degrees, facing away from shore, and after fifteen minutes gain a little breathing room. We turn the bow forty-five degrees back toward land and make good gains until the black cliffs loom over us again. We keep doing this, zigzagging in and out from shore, clawing forward as we can, until finally a foaming sand shoal presents an option. On the other side of the shoal are calmer waters. There appears to be one section of the sandbar where waves aren't breaking as aggressively across its surface as elsewhere. I've lost track of how long we've been working, but Frank and I are worn out. We turn the nose of the *Arctic Joule* and make for the opening. I yell to the cabin to lift the rudder at exactly the right moment, and we scud across the sand and into protected waters. After tossing the anchor, I pull in the oars and head straight into the cabin.

"Good job, guys," Denis says as we enter. "Way to keep it together out there. That's class."

It's raining hard now and the wind is howling, but we're in the cabin and out of the maelstrom. There's not much room to fumble about and change out of our suits, though Paul and Denis aren't fussed. The cabin is a terrible moisture trap and our wet gear isn't helping. When all the hatches are sealed, there's no ventilation, and it would be easy to imagine us falling off to sleep and never waking up. Fortunately, we can lock the two large hatches leading into the aft cabin—one off the deck and one off the top of the compartment—while still leaving a small gap to the outside. This is essential for the integrity of the locked door in the event of a mishap. The single biggest danger for an ocean rowing craft is to have water flood into the cabin and upset its balance.

Four months ago, an ocean rowing expedition traversing the Atlantic made international news after a rogue wave flushed through an open hatch into their cabin while the team was making a shift change. The wave capsized their boat and, once flipped, the boat wouldn't re-right. The team was forced to deploy their safety raft and call for rescue. Fortunately, the water they capsized in was warm and cargo ships were plying nearby waters so a rescue was close at hand. A similar situation for us would likely prove fatal. There's no marine traffic in these waters: any possible rescue would be days away. We have an emergency raft on deck and Mustang survival suits, but we're not delusional about our situation. Donning a survival suit and then deploying an emergency raft requires considerable dexterity. Trying to do it in icy water where incapacitation comes rapidly is not a scenario we'd like to test.

"YOU KNOW WHAT I'd fancy now?" Denis says longingly. "An eggs Benny and a yogurt parfait."

"Aha, that would be nice," Paul says. "I'd like a toasted ham, cheese, and onion sangwich." Paul pronounces *sandwich* in a very Limerick way, as my parents do. "That would be savage. Maybe an ol' cappuccino with that, too."

After a few restless hours, the winds subside and we leave our shelter. Low clouds roll in off the ocean. It's much colder now; a stark gloom hangs in the air. A message comes through our satellite phone from Victor, our Russian weather router:

"Congratulations, you've made it to the Amundsen Gulf."

It's a milestone of sorts on a journey where milestones haven't come easy. We round the cape and make it official: the Beaufort Sea is now behind us. We're excited by the moment but sobered by the reality that this next phase brings the ice.

In addition to his words of praise Victor offers words of caution: "Franklin Bay 7/10 ice concentration. Do not enter with your boat." He uses sea-ice codes to describe the ice concentrations ahead. The value 7/10 indicates 70 percent sea ice in 30 percent open water. This ratio is considered "close pack ice" and is no place for any boat other than an icebreaker. Our communication with the Canadian Ice Service confirms his report.

The sea ice sits out in the middle of Franklin Bay and blocks a direct route to its far side at Cape Parry. Franklin Bay is a part of the Amundsen Gulf that, from space, looks like a large pizza slice removed from the pie of the Arctic coast. It's roughly seventy-five miles across the top, from Cape Bathurst to Cape Parry, and seventy-five miles in depth. Current ice conditions leave us no choice but to travel south, deep into it, until we find a safe point at which to cross.

The wind builds again as we head south into Franklin Bay, but this time, for the first time, it's square at our back. Small ice floes are everywhere but we have little difficulty negotiating a path around them. By end of day we're virtually sailing down the coast, our rowing motion simply a gesture adding little to our overall speed.

VIDEO DIARY, DAY 20

DENIS (*laughing*): Banged it out like fucking heroes. Even in our state of exhaustion, we were heroic.

PAUL (*laughing*): At least that's what we're going to tell ourselves we were.

DENIS: Very excited, fucking... ahhhh... fuck... We'll do it again. No swearing.

PAUL (*laughing*): No one's ever going to see these video diaries. Seriously though, this is where you don't know if you're going to make it. This is the real stuff. It depends on the weather, it depends on variables and a bit of luck. This is what it's all about; this is what we've signed up for.

DENIS: Okay, here's the deal: We left Bathurst Point this morning, and in the last six hours we have done thirty-eight kilometers. This is way more like it. This is the kind of figures we know we can do only in the very best weather conditions and we have them right now. We're charging big time and making up for some lost time. We're coming up on the Smoking Hills, which I didn't think we'd get to for a couple days, never mind six hours.

IN 1826, NATURALIST John Richardson traveled these shores and charted this landscape for the first time as a member of John Franklin's second overland expedition to find the Northwest Passage. Franklin and Richardson journeyed down the Mackenzie River together and parted ways at the delta. Franklin traveled west to Alaska to see what he'd find, while Richardson traveled east. On his journey, Richardson rounded Cape Bathurst as we did, traveling down Franklin Bay as we're doing right now. Midway down the bay, he discovered something strange, a unique geological phenomenon as bizarre in the Arctic as an iceberg in the desert. He discovered a frozen landscape on fire, and named it the Smoking Hills.

Almost two centuries later, the Smoking Hills remain exactly as Richardson first saw them—mountainsides of billowing smoke that appear as swaths of an unhindered forest fire burning without the forest. The hills contain a stratum of hydrocarbons (oil shale) that is auto-ignited by sulfur-rich lignite deposits within the soil surface. Plumes of gray smoke, similar in look and smell to the clouds emanating from a volcano, rise from the flanks of the hills. The ground is red, orange, and brown and has the look of a wound unattended. The hills have been burning like this for centuries.

Frank and I are on our shift in the early hours of the morning. The wind has calmed and the sky is painted with charcoal bands of cloud, backlit by the deep orange of a dying Arctic sun. Chunks of ice, contorted into the exotic and the grotesque, float among us, tinged in pink, mirrored on the flat sea. Clouds of smoke rise from the black cliffs of the Smoking Hills and continue to the horizon. I hear a large whooshing sound to my right. Mist rises from the sea and a dark serpent slides above the water to disappear again, the gentle flick of a tail sending it to the depths—a bowhead whale in this Tolkienesque world.

A favorable current and tailwind follow us down Franklin Bay, granting us a staggering seventy-five miles of travel in twenty-four hours of rowing, over double the distance of our previous longest mark, not counting our push down the Mackenzie River. The ice thins at the bottom of the bay and we risk a twenty-one-mile open-water crossing to the Parry Peninsula on the far side. It's a smooth traverse with only a two-mile band of ice debris disrupting our path, but as we near the coast we notice a wall of dark cloud approaching from the northwest. A massive low is currently stalled over the Beaufort Sea, and the periodic gales we've felt over recent days are coming from this monster. It has built-in strength and has just been upgraded to an Arctic cyclone.

We watch the black wall as it approaches but there's little we can do. The shoreline is steep and rocky; it's no place to weather a storm, so we keep moving. Paul and Denis are on the oars when the storm hits. The boat begins to rock wildly as waves pound the hull and send thundering reverberations through the boat. "There's a tiny inlet just up ahead," I scream out to them. "It's about half a kilometer away." I'm looking at the onboard navigation screen in the cabin. All Paul and Denis can see outside is a panel with speed, heading, and depth, but no map. Why we didn't incorporate an exterior screen into our setup is beyond me. The inlet appears, guarded by a series of breaking waves. We hold our breath and push five hundred yards through the foam to the shelter of a tiny gravel lee, as hostile and exposed as a lee can be but offering some protection from the storm. We spend the rest of the evening rocked by the sea, a growling, angry gale our only company.

WE'RE ALL EATING a freeze-dried meal while waiting out the storm when the topic of real food surfaces.

"Bread, garlic bread, and of course chipper chips," Paul says when I ask him what he'd like right now. "Fucking hell, I haven't had a chipper chip since I was in Ireland. And a Coke, of course. This pepper steak isn't bad, all said, but should have put a little more water into it, though." He stirs the spoon inside his freeze-dried food pouch as he talks. "The lasagna is scrumptious, though. Denis is crying over it now, it's so good."

"It's unbelievable," Denis agrees, his mouth half full as he speaks. "I'd say it's one of the nicest dinners so far."

We have 350 or so freeze-dried meals on board and will pick up another bunch when we get to Cambridge Bay. Each meal comes in a sealed packet so boiling water can be poured directly into it, eliminating the need for a bowl. It's as efficient as it can be—add water, wait ten minutes, eat—and we have two such meals allotted for each of us for each day of the journey. There's a wide variety of meals on board—beef stroganoff, pepper steak, pasta primavera, chili mac, lasagna, beef stew, chicken vindaloo with rice, pad thai, Santa Fe chicken, chicken teriyaki with rice, three-bean chili, vegetable curry with rice, Katmandu curry, mac and cheese, Jamaican barbecue chicken—and we select them at random. The meals are stored in a hatch under the rowing deck, and each time we finish a shift we unscrew the sealed hatch lid, stick an arm down, and grab a couple of pouches. We get what we get; it's always a surprise. We've been storing all our food in these hatches but recently removed the oatmeal because the fiberglass fumes from the hull were working their way through the paper walls of the packets. Even though they were all stuffed inside large Ziploc bags, they had the distinct taste of fiberglass once cooked, and after the first time I tried one, I insisted we discard everything that had been exposed. No one else seemed particularly concerned, but I figured if you could taste fiberglass, you were ingesting it, and that's definitely not good.

By six in the morning the storm has passed and we move again. The sea has become glass smooth and a misty fog hangs in the air. Frank and I remain close to shore to keep things visually interesting, but the barren landscape of the Parry Peninsula is far from stimulating. There's little vegetation now; low-lying benches of barren rock provide the only scenery. As we round a small headland, a splash of color onshore catches my eye. It's a mere speck, really, a little blob of yellow, but any color in this gray landscape pulls you in. This is the first piece of garbage I've seen on these shores other than a rusting oil barrel, and I squint to make out what it is. Scale is difficult to discern in this environment and I'm convinced it's some sort of canvas until I see it move.

"Check out it Frank... over there," I say, pointing to shore. "That yellow thing there. I think it saw it... There again. It moved."

We swing the bow of the *Arctic Joule* to starboard and start heading toward shore. The yellow blob takes shape and we soon realize it's a person moving back and forth over a ridge, coming in and out of view.

"I don't think they see us," Frank says, as the person disappears. The closer we get to shore, the clearer everything becomes.

"There's a kayak there too," I say, "and I think that's a tent poking out over the ridge."

A faint gray wash of smoke starts to rise from behind the ridge. When we're about 150 feet from shore, the yellow figure reappears and notices us. The shoreline drops off deeply, and once we anchor, we need to jump into the ocean and swim a few strokes before finding our feet and scrambling onto the beach.

"I didn't expect to see anyone out here," says a petite woman with a broad smile.

"Us, too," I reply.

"We'd heard about you in Inuvik. The solo woman kayaker," Paul says. "How are things going?"

Her name is Diane Haché, and she started her kayak journey in Inuvik a couple of weeks before we did.

"I'm having a few issues," Diane says, shrugging. "I've been having trouble finding fresh water the last few days."

Diane's being modest in articulating her troubles. We quickly discover that her satellite phone is out of battery and she has no way of recharging it; her dry suit has a large zipper stuck open, making it useless if she dumps into the water; her kayak is cracked and leaking; her shotgun is rusted; her only real food is noodles and rice, although she has a few dried meals for emergency; and now she has no fresh water.

"I drank the water in the lagoon back there," she says, pointing to the small body of water on the other side of the ridge. "It tasted salty, though."

"That's ocean water," Frank says. "You can't drink that. It'll destroy your kidneys."

We spend the next hour sitting around a driftwood campfire and learn this is Diane's second journey into the Arctic.

"I paddled the Mackenzie River three years ago," she says. "The RCMP stopped me along the way and wouldn't let me continue unless I carried a satellite phone. My family was worried about me. I got a phone in the end and kept going."

Diane's appearance completely belies her reality. She's a mother of four adult children with a vitality that exceeds a woman half her age.

"I'm fifty-eight feeling like thirty," she says, laughing.

An Acadian from Bathurst, Nova Scotia, she now lives in Yellowknife, N.W.T., where she works as a miner. This tiny, attractive mother of four is not what I'd imagine as an Arctic miner but, then again, she's not what I'd imagine as a solo-expedition Arctic kayaker either.

"I'd like to get to Kugluktuk, you know... Coppermine... but who knows," she says with a smile. "I go with the flow."

Frank manages to fix Diane's dry suit with zipper oil from our kit and I fill up all her water containers with fresh water from our boat. We donate a few cherished chocolate bars as well as several dehydrated meals and let her charge her phone from our batteries. As we row away from her campsite, I'm struck by the boldness of her effort. Her safety net is poor at best, and if anything goes wrong, she could be in a terrible way. There's a fine line between boldness and recklessness, and she's straddling that line. I feel genuine concern for her.

"She's hanging it out there," Denis says as we row out from shore. "Did you see the state of that shotgun?!"

We slip away from shore and give Diane a final wave. Frank and I row for the remainder of our shift. The seas remain calm as we hand things over to the boys.

I'M ASLEEP WHEN the storm hits. Paul and Denis have almost completed an exposed nine-mile traverse from one headland to another when a gale-force wind smacks the boat broadside, pushing it so hard, the boys are unable to keep a straight line. Before they know it, the *Arctic Joule* is being swept into the open waters of Sellwood Bay. As I poke my head out on deck, Paul and Denis are standing up, prepping to come into the cabin.

"What's up, guys?" I ask, confused.

"It's no use," Denis says, pointing to the far shore. "The wind's too strong. We couldn't reach the lee." The boat is moving perpendicular to the direction we want to go.

"We deployed the sea anchor to slow us down," Paul says, "but we're still moving fast."

A sea anchor works like an underwater parachute; depending on its size and drag, it can stop a boat in the water or significantly slow its movement. Our sea anchor is proving too small for this wind and is allowing us to be pushed at half a mile an hour toward the far shore of the bay.

"You guys are almost done," Frank says. "We'll take over."

Frank and I scramble out on deck with dry suits on and start our watch.

"How long is the ground anchor line?" I call out to Paul through the plexiglass hatch.

"Seventy feet or so," his muffled answer comes back.

The navigation screen indicates a current depth of 565 feet. Over the course of the next hour we watch that number slowly decrease as we approach shore. We're about a half-mile out when the magic number 70 appears and we replace slow negative movement with no movement at all.

"It's holding," I say out loud, as the ground anchor grabs hold of the bottom. "Let's head in, I'm exhausted." A quick scan of the horizon indicates clear water, so Frank and I join Paul and Denis in the cabin for some rest.

A peculiar rapping sound against the hull wakes me up. I think it's Denis at first, but he's still asleep, as are the other two. I lie in such a way that I face out the cabin door, able to survey water conditions by just sitting up. With the banging noise I sit bolt upright, but I don't see the churning sea I expect.

"Holy shit!" I shout. "*It's ice!*"

In seconds we're all on deck facing down a hundred-by-hundred-foot ice floe that has wedged itself up against our bow. The storming wind is pushing it hard, moving it directly over top of us. We try to release our anchor, but it's stuck as this multiton piece of ice some forty to fifty feet thick has positioned itself above it, making it impossible to retrieve. We push the bow away and gain a few yards of slack to loosen the anchor, but it's no use. The ice sheet is being pressed against us and we can't move. Our anchor line stretches as taut as a piano wire, and the boat begins to moan under the strain. *The Arctic Joule*'s nose starts to drop, being pulled down by the anchor line and the weight of the moving ice. If we don't do something immediately, we'll be swept under it.

"Where the hell did this thing come from?" I scream. "There was no ice just a couple hours ago."

Even if there had been, we present such a small bull's-eye on such a massive target that the chance of a piece of ice hitting us seemed very remote. Yet somehow this big chunk of ice has found us.

The groaning of the boat and the dipping of the bow leaves me no choice. Like when you have your coattails caught under a steamroller, there's only one outcome here. I pull out the serrated knife from my PFD, crawl to the bow of the boat and cut the anchor line—*ping!* With the touch of the blade, the rope explodes and we spring free.

We're about a half-mile from shore and the wind pushes us in quickly. One dilemma switches to another as we sail headlong toward a rocky beach with no anchor to keep us off it. We're forced to find as smooth a section of beach as possible and head in. The moment the bow of the *Arctic Joule* runs up onto the gravel, we jump out to prevent the stern from swinging broadside to the waves. We take turns standing chest deep in the icy cold water, keeping our bucking bronco from breaking free and breaching. Just when all seems hopeless, another ice floe appears a few hundred yards offshore heading in our direction. This one is smaller than the behemoth we tangled with earlier but still carries enough girth to be imposing. I have an idea.

We make a sharp effort, pushing off from shore and heading into the lee of the incoming ice. It becomes grounded on the seabed, as I'd hoped, and we take the opportunity to use it as moorage. I clamber atop the huge slab, place two ice screws into the surface and rig a satisfactory anchor—in reality, an ice-climbing anchor—and we hold fast. We're in the lee of the ice a short distance from shore and safely out of the wind.

Denis is a fan of the eighties pop rocker Chris de Burgh, and on a number of occasions, after particularly challenging days on this trip, he's threatened to serenade us with a Chris de Burgh classic. Now he's so happy with our mobile ice moorage that he names it Chris the Ice Berg.

Moored to Chris, out of the storm, we breathe deeply after our ordeal and slip into the cabin, but no sooner are we out of our dry suits than we hear a thundering crash outside and a thump against the boat. I poke my head out the rear cabin hatch.

"Fuck!" I yell. "It's disintegrating."

Pounded by the waves, Chris is breaking up and appears ready to somersault. It's still the size of a small building and unfortunately now we're attached to it. After another mad frenzy of donning dry suits, we leap onto the disintegrating berg to free ourselves before being cast back into the breaking surf and winds.

VIDEO DIARY, DAY 23

(*The camera lens is foggy, and it's tough to see Paul and Denis clearly.*)

DENIS: We ran into a massive storm. Erm, we tried to anchor, we got hit by an iceberg, we tried to go to shore, we couldn't get ashore because it was too rough, we managed to ice-screw ourselves onto a landfast piece of ice, which proceeded to break apart, and now we're battling upwind in pretty hectic conditions to find some shelter because there's none around here.

PAUL: Right now we're doing twenty-minute shifts, so twenty minutes on and twenty minutes off, because it's that hard, we're pulling, it's so tiring, like, we're all exhausted, everything's wet, we're cold...

We're all at wits' end and remain on our twenty-minute shifts for the next several hours, just yards from the shore's edge, knowing full well that a submerged rock could puncture the hull and breach the boat. But there's nothing we can do about it: the wind is too strong.

We creep along, fighting for all we're worth, and lose track of time. We're all exhausted when we spot it—a tiny, ice-choked bay. It's not on our charts but we have no choice. The sea calms and the wind dies as we enter. We've lost ground but we're alive.

It's only then that I see the outstretched hand float by.

7
MESSAGE IN A BOTTLE

I'M IN A BIT OF a daze after the last few hours, but now, safely on land, I can reflect on what truly happened out on the water. There's no doubt we survived our ordeal by the skin of our teeth. Had I not woken up when I did, that big piece of multi-year sea ice would have moved right over top of us, sucking us underneath it. I take pride in having anticipated treacherous conditions on previous expeditions and taking steps to mitigate them, but this expedition feels different. I sense the objective dangers of the task are bigger than I anticipated, and in many ways they still remain an unknown. It's a humbling moment.

"Look at that!" Frank exclaims, pointing out into the water. "It's a hand . . . It's the hand of Franklin!"

A large chunk of ice is floating past us about a hundred feet offshore. What looks like a human arm grasping for the sky extends from its surface. A sculptor couldn't have created something more convincing. We all stare at it in disbelief.

"Where the hell did that come from?" Denis says, shaking his head. "It's a bad omen for sure."

It's my first thought too, one I try to dismiss, but there's little denying it. The outstretched arm looks like that of a drowning man grasping for something, anything that will save him. The hand of Franklin indeed.

It's a sobering sight that locks all of us in our thoughts. Paul and I tie the *Arctic Joule* to a large log on the gravel shore—our anchor is gone now—and start unloading gear to dry it out on the beach. Denis and Frank collect driftwood and start building a fire. We'll likely be here for a while.

The small inlet where we're moored is crescent-shaped with several pieces of sea ice nestled into its far side. A sweeping band of gravel separates the ocean from a smaller lagoon beyond, a patch of calm that visually extends our bay backward so it looks like a triangle of water with an arc of gravel through it. To the east, a small hillside of shattered limestone stacked in benches, almost castle-like in form, shelters the bay. I clamber to the top to take in the view and stumble upon two small oval depressions, each surrounded by large pieces of rock. They're both roughly ten feet by thirteen, cut into the hillside as if to garner protection from the wind.

Back in 2007, while we were walking the beaches of King William Island, local historian Louie Kamookak showed me a similar site—a ring of rocks encircling a depression in the ground high up on a slope overlooking the water of the Northwest Passage. It had been dated at four hundred to five hundred years old, yet caribou bones still scattered the floor. "Bones last a long time up here," Louie said, pointing to the pieces. "These are food scraps from their last meals."

It appears our site could be at least as old. Thule tent ring sites found on Cape Parry date back over a thousand years; the location of these two here speak to people seeking respite from the wind and ice, just as we have. The Thule ventured into the Arctic during a warming trend called the Medieval Climatic Optimum between 900 and 1100 AD. They originated from the Bering Strait and moved eastward to Peary Land in northern Greenland over the course of several generations. The Thule were master whale hunters, and a warming Arctic favored their skills. Temperatures rose only a couple of degrees Celsius during that period, but the effects on the ecosystem were profound. The tree line moved north by sixty miles, bringing with it all the associated boreal life, and Arctic waters began to abound with marine mammals. The Thule had discovered an environment teeming with bounty, and quickly displaced the existing and less technologically advanced Dorset culture, either by absorption or force—archaeologists are still unsure— quickly becoming the sole inhabitants of the Arctic. Today, all Inuit people draw a direct lineage from the Thule. It's impossible not to feel a sense of impermanence and mortality while standing in front of these ancient tent rings.

SEVERAL MONTHS AGO, before embarking on this adventure, I decided to share my journey with my two young daughters— Caitlin, nine, and Arianna, seven—in a very special way. I wrote a message to each of them as if I was talking to them in the future, to the two young women I anticipated they'd become. The process proved much more powerful than I'd expected. Tears streamed down my face as I wrote to my children as adults, at a time when I might be gone. I rolled the notes into small scrolls, slipped each one through a claddagh ring—a traditional Irish ring that represents love, loyalty, and friendship and that speaks to our family heritage—and placed them in a small sealed PVC tube. My plan was to hide it somewhere special along this journey.

I have the time capsule with me now. I slip it under a large piece of limestone with a distinctive orange mark, adjacent to one of the ring sites, and take a GPS reading. If my daughters want to retrieve their notes, they'll need to travel north to find them. In the process, they'll experience the Arctic themselves, experience a place that is deeply important to their father, a place that may have profoundly changed by the time they get here.

Emotion wells up in me. I start walking back to the boat. The rest is up to my girls.

DEEP SLEEP COMES easy for all of us, and we awake to calm seas in our refuge bay, with small waves lapping the sides of our boat. The telltale sign of change is the stillness of our cabin, but it's often easy to miss. The gentle rocking of the boat and the merciful silence from the screaming wind keeps us asleep rather than rousing us to work.

But we rally quickly and begin retracing our lost ground across Sellwood Bay, reaching our previous high point within a couple hours. I can't but help think of Diane and hope she was still onshore when that storm hit. The day unfolds nicely, with light winds and comfortable temperatures setting the mood, at least for the moment.

The weather begins to deteriorate on the fourth rowing shift, when offshore riffles build quickly. We're near land as we skirt the inside of a large field of broken ice and make for the best lee we can find. Our options are much more limited now that we've lost our anchor, but we find suitable moorage on a gravel beach and rest until things settle. After the trials of the last thirty-six hours, we are learning to appreciate how quickly things can change up here.

"The hand of Franklin sure slapped us around," Frank says as we hole up in the cabin to wait out the wind. "This boat is so different from anything I've used before; it puts a new kink on things. If you're in a canoe or kayak, you're pretty nimble, you can quickly go anywhere you want. All the beaches here are accessible by kayak or canoe, but because of the specifics of this boat we're severely constrained where we can run and hide."

There's no frustration in his voice, just a matter-of-fact reflection on our reality. *The Arctic Joule* has its limitations.

ALTHOUGH THE WIND dies down by about two-thirty in the morning, the Arctic fog limits our visibility to a mere fifty yards. We lose all sight of land and travel solely by GPS and compass. The seas begin to change as we round Cape Parry, and within minutes the wind has blown up. The invisible walls of the cliff on the cape reflect steep waves at us, which mix with the swell of the gulf and the chop from the wind and push us in circles. We're spinning wildly. A strong current appears in this mix. The wind builds to gale force, pushing us out to sea. We hold a straight line southeast and start rowing hard, away from the crazy waters of the cape, away from land, out into the gulf—right into the path of heavy pack ice.

Our GPS shows a tiny island in our path—a stroke of luck just when we need it. If we can hold our line, we may be able to land. Frank holds a line that will drift us about a half-mile above the island where we can turn and surf our way down to it. We battle cross seas for a tense thirty minutes. The scream of the wind dies as we start to glide with it. "It's like landing a paraglide on a postage stamp," Frank quips. Sitting amid white-capping rollers, we race toward our fog-shrouded island. Paul and Denis come on deck to help us spot.

"We're four hundred meters out," Frank screams. "Do you see anything?"

"Nothing," Paul shouts.

"Two hundred meters out."

"Nothing," Paul yells. "Wait a moment, I think I see—"

We all hear it before we see it: the deep, resonating thud of waves against the steep cliffs of tiny Bear Island. I strain my neck over my left shoulder to see huge waves, little hope. Our island refuge is no salvation at all.

We're traversing sideways, looking for a potential landing point. "Over there!" Paul screams. "Can we land on that?" He's pointing to a steep rocky beach, maybe forty yards wide, totally exposed to the waves, but it's our only choice. As we hit the beach, Paul and Denis leap out and keep the stern perpendicular to the surf. We've found our port for this storm, such as it is.

BY MORNING OUR boat is encased in a slushy porridge with larger chunks of ice groaning around it. Even though these massive pieces of sea ice that move about our island look like icebergs, they're not. The distinction is important. Icebergs are born from the land, huge pieces of ice that have calved from an ice shelf or glacier and slipped into the ocean. Sea ice, on the other hand, is frozen ocean, made from it and eventually melting back into it.

Sea ice acts like a planetary air conditioner, and is critical in moderating our global climate. Satellites monitoring sea-ice growth and retreat across the Arctic since 1978 have shown it in steady decline. Since 2002, the minimum summer sea-ice extents have remained well below the long-term average between 1979 and 2000, and the decline appears to be accelerating.

On September 16, 2007, sea-ice extents dropped to a record low of 1.59 million square miles, a full 24 percent less ice than the previous record minimum, set in 2005, when the Northwest Passage became completely ice-free for the first time in recorded history and remained that way for several weeks. Then, in September 2012, another record was set when minimum ice extents dropped an additional 270,000 square miles below the 2007 minimum. Once again the Northwest Passage became bare of ice, an open waterway from the Atlantic to the Pacific.

Because of its white surface, sea ice reflects most of the sunlight that hits it back into space. It's like wearing a white T-shirt on a summer day. Replace the white T-shirt with a black one, and you'll get a lot warmer. The same goes for the Arctic Ocean. The melting of sea ice leaves a steely dark ocean in its place, a dark medium that absorbs the bulk of sunlight that reaches it. As the Arctic Ocean warms and absorbs more ice, it becomes more difficult for sea ice to form again in the winter, leading to an unrelenting melting cycle and increasing sea-ice decline. Many climate scientists feel we could have an ice-free Arctic as soon as 2030.[1]

The repercussions of this are terrifying. The Arctic may seem distant and surreal for most of us, but as it warms, weather patterns will change and the ramifications of a melting Arctic will come home to roost among us all.

The effect of a warming Arctic on the weather is a little complicated, but not too difficult to understand. Warm air takes up more volume than cold air, with equatorial warm air pushing up higher into the atmosphere than Arctic cold air. This volumetric gradient generates winds that drop lower in the atmosphere from the equator to the Arctic, sliding down an atmospheric slope from their high at the equator to their low in the Arctic. Influenced and accelerated by the spin of the earth, these downslope winds create what we know as the *jet stream*. As the Arctic warms, the gradient between the equatorial high and the Arctic low decreases, and the winds that fall between the two ends of the gradient lessen in force, resulting in a weaker jet stream.

The jet stream is a meandering flow of fast-moving air. Its path, like a river's, is affected by the speed at which it moves, so a fast-moving current flows in a much straighter line than a slow-moving one. As the jet stream flows, it pushes air masses around; as it changes direction, weather patterns change. So the jet stream has a significant impact on climate. Climate scientists are discovering that the decreasing difference between equatorial high and Arctic low is resulting in a weaker jet stream. This, in turn, is producing a much slower-moving and more meandering river of air. That winding river of air is now swinging much more deeply into mid-latitudes—regions between the extremes of the Arctic and the equator—and staying there for longer periods of time. The result is longer and colder winters in some regions, as the jet stream dips south and allows colder Arctic air to spill out, and warmer winters in others, as the opposite holds true in other regions.

But that's not all. At the line where the jet stream swings north, the warm, moist air of the south mixes with the cold Arctic air of the north, and the clash in temperatures produces storms—and the greater the difference between warm and cold, the bigger and more powerful the storms. Not only that but, because the jet stream is moving more slowly, the storms are lasting longer. We're already seeing this play out in eastern Canada and the United States, where the winter of 2014–15 was plagued with record cold temperatures and violent storms. Some outspoken yet poorly informed individuals, such as President Donald Trump, have pointed to these colder-than-normal winters as proof that climate change doesn't exist. Sadly, the opposite is true. As contradictory as it may seem until it's adequately explained, a warming climate in the Arctic can cause a cooling climate in other regions.

A study in the journal *Nature Geoscience* shows this clearly. Led by Jong-Seong Kug of South Korea's Pohang University of Science and Technology, the study investigated possible connections between extreme cold winter weather systems in North America and South Asia and historically low levels of summer sea ice in the Arctic Ocean. Kug and his team demonstrated that the reduced area of sea ice in the Beaufort and Chukchi seas during the summer of 2014 created a blob of warmer air that sat in the lower atmosphere, where it disrupted weather patterns. This blob of warm air meant the jet stream had taken a big northern swing, creating what atmospheric scientist Jennifer Francis of Rutgers University, who studies Arctic ice and its effects on weather patterns, called a "very strong ridge." She explained that, "downstream of that ridge, the effect is like taking a jump rope and giving it a big whip: it creates a big wave further downstream, a southward dip in the jet stream. That means that cold air is able to plunge down into that area from the Arctic, and that's been contributing to these very cold winters in eastern North America."[2]

Although Kug's study demonstrated a clear link between reduced sea ice in the North and changes in the weather farther south, it didn't postulate what will happen when the Arctic Ocean becomes completely ice-free in the summer. In this scenario, which climate scientists think will occur in the next twenty-five to thirty-five years, all bets are off.

"There is so much disturbing evidence coming out these days about the impacts of increasing fossil fuel burning and other human-caused climate change," Francis says. "It's hard to imagine that anyone can just snub their noses at it and say, 'Things are fine—we don't have to do anything.' "[3]

THE SEA ICE surrounding us at the moment is creating more immediate concerns. "We'll need to keep an eye on the boat," Frank says. "If that line snaps, we could lose her altogether."

We've set up our tent on a grassy bench a short distance above the beach, and we're monitoring the boat around the clock. It's barren and desolate on this little island but, for the moment, we're safe and out of the storm. The grass we've camped on is home to a pair of arctic terns, which are dive-bombing us at every opportunity. They clearly have a nest nearby and are none too pleased by our arrival, sweeping down upon us each time we venture anywhere south of our tent. "Don't worry, we mean no harm," Paul calls up to one with a laugh as it flies in close.

With the need for constant surveillance of the boat, we forgo sleep altogether and play marathon sessions of cards instead. We started this a couple of weeks ago when idling between storms, and now it's become something of a habit. Hearts is the game of choice, and Frank is the resident expert. He taught us the game and has been slaughtering all of us—up until now, that is. Denis and I have started to build some tactics and have almost caught up to him. Paul is faring less well. During a typical session, we'll brew up some tea, open a large chocolate bar, and play hearts until one player accumulates a hundred cards and is deemed the loser. The remaining three players—invariably Frank, Denis, and me—tally our numbers to determine our ranking.

After several hours, the *Arctic Joule* is completely locked in ice and going nowhere. Finally able to let down our guard, we decide to catch some shut-eye, but not before Denis takes a little stab at ribbing Paul. Paul met a woman named Lindsey before embarking on this expedition, and he's been making frequent satellite phone calls to her over the last few weeks. Denis has been having a field day with it.

After a call with Lindsey the other night, Paul had just put down the phone when Denis said, "Ah, jeez, there he is. Why don't you just come out and ask her to marry you?"

"Fuck off," Paul said with a laugh. "I'm just giving her a call."

"Lindsey Gleeson ... Now, that has a ring to it," Denis teased. "Have you thought of names for the kids yet?"

It's several nights later and Denis is at it again.

"Paul keeps falling asleep at night saying he's in love with Lindsey," Denis says. "He hardly even knows her, like!"

"Yeah, right," Paul says, now half asleep and turning on his side.

"I wonder if she's pining for you like you are for her?" Denis continues.

"Fuck off, Denear," Paul says, using the nickname he's come to use for Denis. "Go to sleep."

The perpetual daylight at these latitudes makes it tough to sleep for long, and after a short nap Denis leaves the tent in the hope of catching a fish. He brought a fishing rod along and has tried his luck several times but remains empty-handed. He's not his comedic self of late either, having become much more quiet and introspective. He likely needs some personal time. Frank heads out after Denis does and returns shortly with a smooth piece of gray driftwood in his hand.

"Check this out, Kev," he says. "Looks like something from a wooden sailing ship."

"Kinda looks like a rope pulley," I say. It has a rope groove on its end and a medium-sized hole drilled through its center. "I wonder how old it is."

Decomposition is much slower in the Arctic. A piece of wood like this could be very old. We can't help but wonder if it's a piece of wreckage from some long-lost expedition. It's wishful thinking, of course, and something we'll never know. But Frank's discovery piques my interest and I join him exploring. Bear Island is little more than a hundred yards wide, and most of its surface is exposed rock and gravel, with a spattering of low grass dappling the gray canvas green in spots. We discover

↑ (left to right): Paul Gleeson, Frank Wolf, Kevin Vallely, and Denis Barnett at the completion of the expedition in Cambridge Bay.

↑ Paul and Denis pulling hard, rowing into Cambridge Bay.

← Shark mouth freshly painted on the bow of the *Arctic Joule* in Inuvik.

↑ Archway of rock inter-
rupting an otherwise flat,
desolate shoreline.

→ A rare warm day making for
pleasant rowing, with Frank
on the oars.

↓ Holed up in the stern
cabin of the *Arctic Joule* in
Tuktoyaktuk.

Finding tenuous shelter among chunks of ice on the shoreline of Sellwood Bay shortly after cutting our anchor.

↑ Attempting to winch the *Arctic Joule* up high on the rocky beach of Bear Island.

→ Remains of a polar bear leg at Brown's Harbour hunting camp.

↑ Camping on the shoreline of Darnley Bay.

← A curious grizzly bear on the rocky coast of Victoria Island.

↓ The hand of Franklin in Sellwood Bay.

↑ Creating an ice anchor in the lee of Chris the Ice Berg on Sellwood Bay.

→ Arctic fox on Nicholson Island.

↓ Frank enjoying an Indonesian clove cigarette.

Frank with kayaker Diane Haché.

↑ Shelter cabin at Cape Lady Franklin on Victoria Island.

→ Denis cooking food at the Cape Lady Franklin shelter cabin.

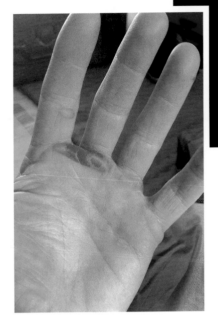

↑ Frank's finger, scalded by spilled boiling water.

← Kevin's blistered hand on day one of the expedition.

↓ Waiting out a storm in the cabin of the *Arctic Joule*.

↑ Nearing the finish in Cambridge Bay.

→ Collecting data for the Department of Fisheries and Oceans with a CTD measuring device.

↓ The Australian team of Matt McFadyen and Cameron Webb anchoring their sailing/rowing boat in the sheltered harbor of Cape Lady Franklin on Victoria Island.

the tiny nest of an arctic tern in one of these grassy areas, a simple depression in the ground with two small, mottled eggs sitting in it in defiance of the hostile world around them.

We see Denis at the edge of a small cliff, rod in hand. His lime green jacket contrasts brightly with the charcoal sea behind him, its surface broiling with foam and froth from the incessant wind. I gaze past him and see a blast of vertical spray erupt from the water, followed by an arc of black as smooth and clean as polished marble, which appears and disappears again.

"There's a whale out there!" Frank says, stealing the words from my mouth. Another geyser bursts from the water, and then another. "There's three of them!"

Bowhead whales are the giants of the Arctic. They're fairly easy to identify from the distinctive pointy blowhole on their head and their enormous size. The three out in the bay are no exception. Bowheads can grow up to sixty-five feet in length and are second only to the blue whale in weight, tipping in at upward of one hundred tons. To put it in perspective, that's the weight of the space shuttle. The bowhead's massive mouth is big enough to park a car in, and makes up fully one-third of its gargantuan body. They're gentle giants that pose no threat to mariners, but you wouldn't want to be on an ice floe with one beneath you. Inuit claim to have seen them surface through two feet of sea ice, using their huge bony skulls as battering rams. Recent studies have suggested some of these behemoths live up to 150 or even 200 years, the longest of any mammal. In 2007, a whale caught off the Alaskan coast was found to have a harpoon head embedded deep in its blubber around its neck. The harpoon was a relic from the whaling days of the 1890s, suggesting that this aged creature was well over a century old.

How climate change will affect the bowhead whale can only be postulated, but changes in sea-ice concentrations, surface temperatures, and ocean currents will all play their part. Warming waters will have an impact on migration patterns and feeding locations, while mortality rates from predation will increase. Bowhead whales, like beluga, use the cover of sea ice to avoid their only nonhuman predator, the killer whale, and a warming Arctic will see not only less protective sea ice but also more killer whales. It's a double-edged sword for this majestic beast.

"Hey, hey, I think I got something!" Denis yells, pulling my attention away from the whales. He hauls on his fishing rod and turns to us with a grin. "I told you I'd get something." He pulls in a blue-green fish with bulging eyes on top of its head, a large downturned mouth, and distinctive fanlike fins.

"It's a ling cod," Frank says. "That'll make good eating!"

Denis heads back to camp with his catch and within the hour has whipped up a delicious meal of fried fish with lemon pepper zest. It's a natural human trait that we appreciate something most when we haven't had it in a while, and fresh food hasn't been on our table in weeks. Our daily routine includes instant porridge for breakfast, PowerBars, chocolate, and beef jerky for snacks, and dehydrated meals for everything else. The freshest thing on our boat since we left Tuk has been the smell of our clothes. This ling cod is a glorious change, and we eat like kings.

OVER THE COMING hours, the storm intensifies, switches direction, and bears directly down on the boat. If not for the surrounding ice moat, the *Arctic Joule* would be destroyed.

The ice and slush that surround her act as a breakwater of sorts, but it won't last long. The relentless pounding of the waves is pulverizing the ice before our eyes, and we're powerless to do anything but watch and hope.

I grew up hearing stories of the Arctic from my dad, who worked for the Department of Transport as a radio operator at the Hopedale Mid-Canada Line station on the northern Labrador coast in 1961–62. On many occasions, he recounted to me how his operations station was destroyed by fire in the middle of winter, and how he and two other employees had to find shelter in a shed until a plane rescued them. The story of his harrowing experience has been with me my whole life, impressing upon me at a young age just how brutal the Arctic environment can be. I lost my dad to cancer just over two years ago, but in recent days, I've felt him close to me, a lone comfort in this hostile world.

I make several calls back home to let family know we're okay. They've been extremely anxious. A blog post I wrote for the *Vancouver Sun* about our anchor debacle several days ago has made the rounds and ignominiously found its way to the front cover of the Thursday edition, the headline screaming, "Last First: Crew Survives Arctic Peril in Close Scrape."

In Ireland, a headline in *The Irish Mirror* exclaiming "Irish Sailors Cheat Icy Death in Arctic Ocean" ratchets the drama meter up even higher. I'm in the midst of writing a blog post about our most recent close call, but thoughts of sensational headlines give me pause as I consider how to frame it.

At two in the morning the wind dies down, gently blowing the sea ice that had encircled the island back into Darnley Bay. Even our little beach is ice-free; the storm lasted just long enough to mash the ice that had enveloped the *Arctic Joule* but somehow left our boat unscathed. The Northwest Passage loosens its grip a hair and we make our escape. You never know what you're going to get up here. We take each day as it comes. Today brings freedom.

8

PAULATUK

VIDEO DIARY, DAY 28

DENIS (*laughing*): You look like a gnome. Like a leprechaun with his beard. Brilliant. Like something you'd see wearing a funny hat on your garden.

PAUL (*looking at Denis, shaking his head, not amused*): Denear, very serious stuff here. (*turning to camera*) We've had a couple hairy days, hairier than our beards.

DENIS (*speaking seriously now*): Things change very quickly here.

PAUL: Things happened. Either one of them could have been the end of the trip... em, possibly the end of something else (*half laughing*). We handled it well.

It's only a three-mile hop from Bear Island to the eastern shore of Parry Peninsula, but the three miles might have been three thousand in recent days, given the impassable morass of ice and wave in our path.

We're all a little anxious upon departure, our nerves ragged after the previous day's troubles, but the rhythm of the rowing eases our minds and before long we're skimming along the east bank of the Parry Peninsula, with Bear Island only a memory.

Our original plan was to cross Darnley Bay directly from Cape Parry to Cape Lyon, but the white line sitting on the horizon indicates that sea ice is still blocking our route, and the Canadian Ice Service report concurs. A finger of 70 percent pack ice pushing down the far coast is blocking our path. The hamlet of Paulatuk sits at the south end of Darnley Bay. We hadn't planned to stop there, but the proximity of the pack ice and the need to replace our anchor forces a change in plans.

VIDEO DIARY, DAY 28, CONTINUED

DENIS: We're about eighty-eight kilometers from Paulatuk, and in town we've got to go and get a new anchor and supplies and we're very excited because we're going to get things like bread and some crisps [potato chips] and little treats that we don't have.

PAUL: Maybe some rashers [bacon] for the sandwiches!

The steep cliffs of Cape Parry have given way to a gentle shoreline of gravel and stone. Small blankets of olive-colored scrub dot a starkly monochromatic canvas of gray rock. It's more difficult to discern beauty here than in the lushness of the mid-latitudes. Words reflecting the richness, vitality, and color of a warmer world don't pepper descriptive verses about the Arctic. Here, beauty is less tangible, defined by the simplicity, fragility, and rawness of the environment. It takes time for my southern sensibilities to see it.

We're only near land a few minutes when we spot a small cabin on the rocky shore, the first artificial shelter we've seen since leaving Tuktoyaktuk almost a month ago, other than the creepy DEW Line stations. Swinging in for a closer look, we see three aluminum motorboats pulled up on the beach and two men standing near them are looking out at us. One of them gives us a big wave, and our eagerness to meet other human beings draws us in. I notice a yellow kayak as well.

As we pull to shore, brothers Joe and Steve Illisiak introduce themselves, welcoming us to their camp. "There's hot coffee inside," Steve says, pointing to the cabin, a single-story gray plywood box with a large radio antenna in front. "We glassed you guys [saw us with binoculars] from way out. We wondered if you were coming in."

Hot coffee to a weary rower is like creamed honey to a hungry bear, and we stumble over one another heading in. The cabin is dark and bare, with an old couch, an aluminum table with chairs, several cots, and a small kitchen counter. The five men inside are quick to welcome us. The genuineness of people in the North, a kind of hospitality I've experienced before in Alaska and Yukon, washes over me here, too.

"Please, there's coffee here, noodles and soup over there, take what you want, make yourself at home," says a big man with a wide toothless grin who's sitting at the far end of the table. "My name's Hank," he says. "Welcome to Brown's Harbour." The confidence of his body language makes it clear he's the boss in this room. As I learn later, his last name is Wolki. There are very few names in the Arctic, so he might be a member of the prominent and widely respected Wolki family, but I don't know how he might be related to Fred, whom we met in Tuk, or his father, Jim, whose exploits played such a significant role in establishing Canadian sovereignty in this part of the Arctic.

Diane is here too, sitting by one of the cots and looking very tired.

"I saw your yellow kayak on the beach," I say. "How did you manage with that storm?"

"I was onshore for it," she says. "I was able to portage around Cape Parry. I'm having a lot of trouble with the crack in my boat."

"I'm happy you're safe," I say. "I was worried for you out there."

I tell her the hair-raising tale of our last couple of days, and we commiserate for a while.

Brown's Harbour is a beluga whaling station, and everyone present here is a resident of Paulatuk. Joe explains to me that the crescent-shaped bay we're situated on is a perfect hunting spot for belugas. "When we see them surface at the point out there, we head out and coral them into this dead-end bay."

Curious about the hunt, I ask a lot of questions. Joe is a little reluctant to answer at first, probably recognizing that a graphic description might be upsetting, but he eventually explains it all. "We force them in shallower waters with our boats," he says. "We then harpoon them through the blowhole when they come up for air. We shoot them then."

Beluga hunting is brutal—there's no sugarcoating it—but it's essential for these people. "The cost of living up here is crazy," Steve says. "Without the country food, an average guy wouldn't make it. It's too expensive."

I joke about how I've been craving a can of Coke and how I'd like to buy a case when we get to Paulatuk.

A man leaning back against the painted plywood wall of the cabin says, "Pop costs you $4.50 a can in Paulatuk."

"A jar of peanut butter is nineteen dollars," another man says. "Maybe your cravings will remain just that."

The people of the North have always harvested food from the land and sea, and likely always will. The grotesquely overpriced "Western" foods found in remote northern villages are more an aberration than a regular part of their diet. Few people can afford the exorbitant costs and, even if they could, the selection is limited and nutritionally poor. Foods shipped to the North are typically chosen for their minimal weight and long shelf life, which means they're generally heavily processed. Except for an annual late-summer barge delivery of large goods, every item not manufactured in an Arctic community needs to be shipped in by air. Fresh fruit and vegetables are rare commodities and when offered come at alarming prices. On my visit to Gjoa Haven in 2007, I saw a half watermelon selling for fifty dollars. What's been called the "country" food of the North has proven to be far healthier for the people, and it's here for the harvesting.

I speak to this from a seemingly contrarian perspective. I've been a vegetarian for over three decades and eschew eating meat in my daily life but, as an urban dweller, that's a luxury I can afford. Up here, meat and fish make up the bulk of an Arctic dweller's diet because there's little else to forage. Vegetarians like me would last only as long as their fat stores would carry them. Both for health reasons and cultural politeness, I decided on my first big adventure back in 2000, when I skied Alaska's Iditarod Trail, to eat anything that was offered to me, and I've abided by this decision ever since. Today beluga is on the table.

Beluga can be eaten raw, cooked, or fermented. The fermented skin and blubber of a beluga whale, or *muktuk,* appears to be the hands-down favorite among my hosts—evidently, it tastes like hazelnut—but it's not on offer today. I'm a little nervous when Hank offers me a piece of raw meat and blubber with a dash of salt, but everyone in the cabin is smiling and laughing. "Go on," Hank says. "It won't bite you." I slip the meat into my mouth, expecting the worst. The blubber has the consistency of butter, while the meat is tough like sinew, and it tastes a bit like ham.

Walking around camp, I notice bones from what was once a very large animal. "Polar bear," Steve says. "Ten-and-a-half-footer. I shot him in the spring." I try to imagine this animal standing on its hindquarters. The rim of a basketball net is ten feet in height and I've never been able to jump and touch one, even with a running start. I picture this monster and my heart moves into my throat.

"Are there many around?" I ask with feigned nonchalance.

"They're probably all out on the ice," one of the younger men says, "but you never know."

THE WIND IS strangely quiet, a sign for us to keep moving. Good travel is proving as rare as vegetation up here, so we bid adieu to our new friends and begin rowing south to Paulatuk. The wind picks up sharply, and it's not long before Diane appears at our stern and bears down on us like we're standing still. She told us she intended to leave shortly after us and she's caught us already. As she passes us, the reality of the *Arctic*

Joule's ineffectiveness becomes glaringly clear. Diane is not a powerful paddler, and she isn't paddling hard, yet she's moving at over double our speed. Even with two of us rowing as hard as we can, we could never match the speed of a kayaker moving into a wind. The windage the *Arctic Joule* presents is simply too great to overcome. Diane disappears ahead of us as the wind builds, and before long we're battling it and going nowhere.

Denis's mood has shifted. Diane's ease in passing us had put him in an angry funk, and we're all feeling it. I'm discovering he's a guy who wears his emotions on his sleeve; if he's happy, we're all laughing, but if he's down, we all stay clear. He's now reluctant to pull out of the wind, so he and Paul keep rowing in place until the hopelessness of the situation becomes obvious. He's so impatient that he even suggests we make a beeline to the far shore of Darnley Bay, knowing full well pack ice is sitting there. Steve Illisiak told us hunters on the far shore reported ice as far as they could see yesterday. It's no place to be at the moment, and we need an anchor anyhow. I understand his sense of frustration and powerlessness, but forcing things when conditions aren't right is simply asking for trouble, which we've found lots of already without seeking it out.

We tuck into a small horseshoe-shaped inlet lined on both sides by blocky brownstone cliffs that look like gatekeepers to the tiny gravel beach that lies beyond. As soon as we enter the bay, the water calms and we glide into its protective embrace. The water here is pristine, its translucence only slightly tinged by a wash of copper green. A thick mist hangs over us, obscuring everything beyond the outer cliffs. We set up our Helsport tent to wait out the wind.

But as reassuring as the hold of this little bay is, the energy among us isn't great. Denis's moodiness is affecting us all, and Diane's unintentional demonstration of the *Arctic Joule*'s limitations isn't helping. In a few weeks, when we're fifty miles from land and the wind is picking up, we'll be whistling a different tune, but right now the lighter and faster kayak is far more appealing. Of course, if not for the ice in Franklin and Darnley bays, we would have rowed straight across the top of each, something a kayaker would likely never risk. That would have saved us hundreds of miles. But we've drawn a bad year—we could have easily done this last year, with its record low ice—and feeling angry won't help. We just have to accept our reality and do the best we can.

THE WIND HOLDS strong for the night and is kind to us in the morning. The mist lifts to reveal calm seas set against cerulean blue skies, and we're drawn out again to dance between tranquility and chaos.

The coastline of the Parry Peninsula extends southward from its tip for roughly thirty miles before it jogs east nine miles to Clapperton Island, just off its tip, and then turns south again toward Paulatuk for another twenty-five. If we follow the coastline we'll paddle thirty miles south and then nine miles east before heading south again. If we aim straight for the tip of Clapperton Island and follow the hypotenuse of the triangle, it won't be as far. It seems a straightforward decision, and we choose to cut the corner and head straight for the eastern edge of Clapperton Island. It's only as we move farther away from land that we realize the unpredictable winds here are playing havoc with our minds. This is a simple crossing, no big deal for the vessel we're rowing in, but the waters here make even a straightforward traverse feel tenuous. The winds on the Northwest Passage build more quickly than anything I've ever experienced before; it often feels like someone flicks a switch and turns on a gale that hits without warning, leaving no time for escape. A strong westerly or southwesterly wind at this point on our crossing would blow us off course, pushing us directly toward the pack ice on the opposite shore of Darnley Bay. Staying close to land gives us a fighting chance against an unfavorable wind, allowing us to find the protection of a bay, or to drop anchor if we had one, but it isn't always convenient. In this case, following the coastline would have required an additional six miles of rowing. We're tired and frustrated and eager to get to Paulatuk, and we make the crossing regardless.

Being perpetually exposed to uncertainty and danger doesn't make one numb to it but rather more accustomed to it. A stressful one-off experience has a way of building up anxiety and tension—making a speech in front of a large audience, for example, or sitting down for an important interview—but repeating this experience over and over either allows you to deal with it better or eventually unhinges you altogether. So far we remain fully hinged, but cracks are showing.

We row continuously for the next twenty-seven hours, rounding Clapperton Island and traveling down the edge of the peninsula as a northeasterly builds. Paulatuk sits at the foot of Darnley Bay, in the middle of a fifteen-mile east–west section that forms the bay's bottom end, and we claw east toward it. The seas push and shove, manhandling us like concertgoers inadvertently caught in a mosh pit, but I'm enjoying the discord. There's no ice here, there's little threat to us or the boat, and my iPod has shuffled together a great stretch of songs. I've noticed over the years that I only connect with the lyrics of songs when my emotions are in a corresponding place—a sad song at a blue time, a contemplative song at a time of introspection. The haunting vocals of Merry Clayton build into the Rolling Stones classic "Gimme Shelter" and it sweeps me away.

The waves gradually lessen and the town of Paulatuk appears on the horizon. We're eager to get to shore, and make a beeline for the hamlet, only to realize that a shallow sandy shoal extends across the mouth of the bay on which the tiny community sits. As the crow flies, the distance is traversable in minutes, but it takes us well over an hour to make a circuitous jog around the shoal, a final test of Denis's ever-thinning patience.

"The speed we're going is a disgrace," he declares as we slip onto a sandy section of shoreline and tie ourselves off to various objects scattered about the beach. "We can't spend much time here." Frustration tinges his words. "We need to get going right away."

I feel his sense of urgency—we all do—but his turn in mood since Diane passed us is grating on us all. Frank and I have talked about it several times, and I even heard Paul exchange a few sharp words with Denis on a recent shift; it's the first time on the trip I've seen the even-keeled Gleeson express anger.

It's one o'clock in the afternoon on Saturday, August 3, and we've been on our journey for almost a month now. Paulatuk wasn't part of the original plan, but neither was an incessant northeasterly, a tug-of-war with a multiton piece of sea ice, or a blind traverse to a rocky inlet in the midst of gale with do-or-die consequences. The only predictable thing on any adventure is that unpredictable things will happen.

The temperature has risen significantly in the last few hours, and we shed our rowing clothing before walking into town. A swarm of mosquitos hover over us as we make our way up a short sandy spur leading to a gravel road that runs the length of the hamlet. I take Paul aside and ask him to speak with Denis. "He's really pissing everyone off," I say. "It can't go on like this."

"I'll see what I can do," Paul says. "I've spoken to him a bit already." If Paul's positivity can't do it, nothing will.

Small wood-clad buildings line both sides of the dirt road and march southward in an orderly procession. A young boy coasts by on his bike, looking like a gangster with his black hoodie pulled over his head, sneaking a few glimpses in his not-so-subtle reconnaissance.

"Where's Hank Wolki's house?" I call out as he cycles away.

"It's that house there," he says, pointing to a brown, lopsided home a couple of buildings away.

Hank Wolki mentioned to us up at Brown's Harbour that his wife, Marlene, runs a B&B out of their home in Paulatuk, and we arranged to spend the night there when we arrived. Like every other home in the community, Hank's is a simple, single-story, rectangular building raised above grade on pylons and capped with a metal gabled roof. A plain wooden staircase leads to an enclosed vestibule and marks the entry to the house. Christmas lights dangle from the eaves. We walk up the steps and rap on a half-open door. Frank leans in and calls out, "Anyone home?"

"Who's there?" a female voice asks. A heavyset woman with a round face and beaming smile greets us at the door. "Hi, my name is Marlene. You must be the boaters. Hank said you'd be arriving."

As I step inside, I notice Hank in the kitchen just over Marlene's shoulder. "Hey, guys, come on in," he says.

"Would you like some coffee?" Marlene asks. "Come in, have a seat." Marlene directs us to the living room and sets about making our coffee, but both Frank and I are immediately drawn to the kitchen, where huge chunks of meat are spread out all over the floor. The meat is beluga, harvested at Brown's Harbour a few days earlier, and has the distinctive cross section of white skin atop two inches of white blubber with pink flesh beneath. It's cut into chunks and strips and lies on sheets of cardboard.

"Sorry about all this," Hank says, "but we need the space to prepare the meat."

Chunks of meat boil away in a big aluminum pot on the stove, and strips of beluga are piled high in a blue plastic bin on the floor. "We're making muktuk," Hank explains. "We place the beluga meat in the bucket and let it ferment for a week. We need to stir it, though, three times a day, or it will go rancid. It's delicious when it's done!"

The Wolki family is one of the preeminent Inuvialuit fur-trapping families of the Western Arctic, and Hank carries his important lineage with ease. He exudes a level of calm and confidence that bespeaks a role as the alpha in town. "He's the man for sure," Frank observes astutely. Marlene's brother, Chris, drops by the house and talks of Hank in a manner that confirms our reading. "When you hunt with Hank," he says, "you try to keep up, and if you manage to keep up, you learn lots." We're not surprised to find out that Hank is the snowmobile champion of Paulatuk, and has the fastest sled and the nicest boat.

Hank and Marlene's house is a welcome respite for us and provides an opportunity to wash our clothes, take a hot shower, and connect with family and friends. Denis seems to be coming around as well. He's spoken with friends in Ireland, and their words of encouragement have buoyed his spirits. "They think what we're doing is hardcore," he says, clearly feeling better. "They think what we've done so far is class."

I see that Denis, being on his first expedition, is very concerned about how people are perceiving what he's doing. I understand. I remember the same feeling on my first expedition to Alaska, back in 2000. Although I still care to a degree, I've learned through experience that you can't let outside pressures get the better of you, no matter how intense they are. We've been the target of some really nasty attacks on social media and—I won't lie—it's irked me. It's taken everything I have not to lash out, and an undercurrent of nastiness continues to foul the waters of our communication.

"The #AGW [anti–global warming] cult idiots are still trying to row the NW passage. Hilarious," tweets @gdthomp01_bkup.

"Oh well, the best laid plans of adventurers, Eco Greenie Kool Aide Chuggers and morally superior folks are often upset by reality," Fred from Canukistan tweets.

Traitor in Chief slides in a racist undertone when he writes, "Well, now the draggers can book a room at madam mukluks Bearhug Inn."

Some comments suggest we're being towed, others that we have a secret motor on board. One individual, sitting in the warm comfort in front of his or her computer screen somewhere, declares us "chicken's of the sea" [sic] because we won't row headlong into the pack ice, while another tells us to save ourselves and give up while we still can. A person named @oeman50 tries to use a little irony in his comment, but his plan backfires when he writes, "According to WikiP, the name Paulatuk means 'place of coal' in the local vernacular. Oh, the ironing..." I want to assure him that our clothes are wrinkle-free, but we promised each other not to engage these comments, no matter how deliciously tempting.

Most significantly, the loud voice of anti-climate-change zealot Steve Goddard is maintaining his rant in a series of blog posts about our trials over recent weeks as well as in tweets. In a taste of his imbalanced commentary, he writes, "They are probably being driven to madness by 'green' scumbags with a profit agenda." All we can do is keep moving forward and do what we're doing to the best of our abilities. We'll never silence our detractors, and we won't stoke their fires by trying.

In the context of all this anonymous questioning and ridicule, I ask Hank and Marlene for their thoughts on climate change and what they've experienced over the years. "Climate change is happening, there's no doubt," Marlene says unequivocally. "The bay in front of Paulatuk was always frozen in early October, but now it's always open. We were picking berries in early September last year too. We've never done that before."

Hank talks about it from the perspective of a hunter out on the ice. "It doesn't get thick anymore," he says. "Today when you hunt the polar bear you have to be very, very careful. The ice is always opening up. Twenty years ago it was so thick, I remember you couldn't even find an open lead or open water." He explains to us how orca are now appearing in the waters too, something they've never seen before. "Killer whales are new for us; we know nothing about them. They're scaring the smaller animals into the bays. We used to have to go out to the ocean to hunt seals, but they are coming into the bay now. It was never that way before."

I'm struck by the disconnect between the rhetoric being spat at us and the experiences of people who actually live in the Arctic. Everyone we've spoken to so far talks of huge change here, of a fundamental shift in climatic conditions, yet their voices are being ignored.

There are the climate change deniers who resist change because they recognize that steps to address it will affect them negatively. No argument will sway them because they don't want to be swayed, but fortunately they're the minority. The individuals we hope to sway are not the ill-willed or selfish but those who remain skeptical about the science. An ice-free Northwest Passage speaks to the dramatic changes befalling the Arctic. Our detractors point to our difficulties to date as proof that there is no problem in the Arctic. But anyone who makes even a small effort to understand the science recognizes, if anything, that our struggles with the increasingly anomalous Arctic weather supports our position. The real voice of climate change in the Arctic comes from the people who live here, and the voices we've heard so far have been very clear. The most important thing we can do is bear witness to the changes they're living with daily and share them with the world as best we can.

ON A WHIRLWIND tour of town, we chat with locals and soak up the friendly vibe. This is a nice place. The population of Paulatuk is just over three hundred, and when strangers are in town, it doesn't take long for word to travel. We pay a much anticipated visit to the Northern store and load up on food we've been dreaming about for days. It's nothing special—a loaf of Wonder Bread, a couple of packs of processed cheese and sliced meat, a bottle of mustard, and a jar of mayonnaise—but it's a culinary feast in comparison to our normal dried-food diet. I've been craving a cold can of Coke, as well; it costs me $3.75.

We heard there were two kayakers in town who arrived just ahead of us, and we're eager to meet them. I'd corresponded with them before starting our expedition and had reports a week ago that they were over a hundred miles behind us, so I'm surprised at how quickly they've caught us. Are we really moving that slowly? We discover them roaming the aisles of the Northern store, like us, disheveled and unkempt as anyone would who'd just stepped in from the wild. Their names are Sébastien Lapierre and Olivier Giasson, they look to be in their early thirties, and they're traveling by double kayak. They're speaking to each other in French when we approach them.

"You guys must be the kayakers," I say, extending a hand in greeting. After we exchange introductions, I ask when they passed us.

"We never did," Sébastien, the more talkative of the two, says. "We portaged the Parry Peninsula, between Franklin Bay and Darnley Bay. It saved us lots of time."

"Wow," I say, shaking my head. "That explains it. I couldn't figure out how you caught us so quick."

Their shortcut avoided the Parry Peninsula and Cape Parry altogether, a 30-mile portage cutting roughly 125 miles off their overall distance. Portaging the *Arctic Joule* is an impossibility, of course. Winching her up onto a steep beach is hard enough; moving her would be a task fit for a pyramid builder. We're envious, of course, but a portage is not something we'd choose even if we could. Our objective is to paddle the Northwest Passage to prove Arctic waters are becoming ice-free. Traveling overland would defeat our purpose.

We ask around town about the arrival of a solo woman kayaker, but everyone shakes their head. This concerns us, as we haven't seen Diane since she passed us just after Brown's Harbour. She should be here now. There's still perpetual daylight up here, so there's no passing in the dark. We can only hope she took shelter somewhere onshore and we missed her as we rowed farther out in Darnley Bay around Clapperton Island. We mention our concern to Hank, and he says he'll keep an eye out and travel up the coast if she doesn't arrive within a few days.

Hank also points us to a supply of scrap steel that we jury-rig together to form the semblance of an anchor—two, actually. They won't be as effective as the real thing, but they're better than nothing, and having two will ease the uncertainty.

Local people come by to pay us a visit. Nurse Norma Hickey and counselor Stephanie Leithead (who's from Vancouver) bake us a cake. We also get a drive up to the dump to spy a mother grizzly and cub, but when we arrive the bruins are nowhere to be seen.

Evenings are starting to cool and darken now; on recent nights, the sun has dropped to the edge of the horizon. Twilight paints everything with a yellow wash, enhancing the warmth of the landscape while increasing its sense of depth with the sharp contrasts of elongated shadows.

We get a good night's rest at the guesthouse and wake early to prepare for our departure. We're all drinking strong coffee when Hank enters the living room through the front door. "I hope all the commotion didn't wake you up this morning," he says. "There was a house fire in town. Had to take care of it. No one hurt, thank God."

"What happened?" I ask.

"Some kids were partying in a house down near the Northern. The owners are out of town. It's badly damaged now."

"I take it fire-fighting duties are a communal thing around here?"

"No," Hank says. "I'm the deputy fire chief."

"Of course you are," I mumble to myself. Hank Wolki, I think, smiling—Paulatuk's man in charge.

9

THE BEACHES OF
THE DOLPHIN AND
UNION STRAIT

WE LEAVE PAULATUK IN THE early evening hours on a dying
south wind. As we slip away, Paul and Denis memorialize our
visit.

VIDEO DIARY, DAY 30

PAUL: Paulatuk was class. We got to eat something other than
dried food for the first time in a month. Myself and Denis had
been talking about a crisp sandwich for two days leading up to
it. We got a loaf of sliced bread, a load of crisps, mayonnaise,
mustard, cheese, a few cans of Coke, sat down by the boat...
delicious! The old fellas did the same. It was savage.

DENIS: We stayed with two local people, Hank and Marlene,
absolute legends. We walk in and there's half a beluga whale on
the kitchen floor. (*Laughing and shaking his head.*) They had a
freezer full of animals that still look like animals.

PAUL: We're headed up to Cape Lyon now. It's about seventy-five kilometers away. It's nine o'clock now, so we'll probably be there some time tomorrow.

Sandbars guard the exit to Paulatuk and we need to make a three-mile detour before setting our heading to the far eastern shore of Darnley Bay and to Cape Lyon beyond. Our intent is to cut the large corner of the bay with a straight-line traverse of Darnley Bay, but the idea quickly shows its weakness. A southerly wind has started to build, and the deeper waters of the traverse will prevent us from using our ground anchor if we need it. Without a ground anchor, we'll be limited to our sea anchor to slow us down and, as we discovered the hard way in Sellwood Bay, our sea anchor still allows enough drift that if it blows hard for twelve hours—not an unlikely scenario—we'll be right back where we were three days ago.

We decide to head closer to shore and take the longer coastal route in shallower water so we can better control our movement. This proves to be a wise decision as over the next twenty-four hours we deploy our ground anchor twice, both times to halt the aggressive push of a twenty-knot southeasterly that would have blown us right out into the middle of the bay. The wind eventually dies and we're able to row continuously to Cape Lyon in a twenty-six-hour burst, which allows us to claw back some lost time.

When people of the North travel, whether on land or water, it's typically to hunt. The concept of leisure travel is lost on them, and for good reason. Travel here is dangerous and done out of necessity. A broken-down car for a person down south means a frustrating delay and a tow truck, but a broken-down boat or snow machine in the Arctic could mean a life-or-death turn of events.

Humans rarely use most of the route we're traveling—there's no reason to—and as a result we have a unique opportunity to observe it. Before leaving on this expedition we partnered with the Vancouver Aquarium and the Department of Fisheries and Oceans. They tasked us with collecting ocean data along our route so ocean scientists might get a better picture of what's happening in the waters of the Northwest Passage. They gave us a special device that measures a host of different ocean characteristics, including conductivity, temperature, and depth—hence, the devices' name: CTD. The Department of Fisheries and Oceans has very little CTD information from the Northwest Passage, so any data we collect will act as a benchmark for future observations.

Deploying the CTD is fairly straightforward but still requires effort and commitment, especially when conditions are not ideal, which is most of the time. The device itself is roughly three feet long and four inches in diameter, with several black rubber hoses emanating from a hard, white plastic cylindrical body. It's clipped to a downrigger affixed to the boat and is steadily lowered to the ocean floor. A five-pound lead ball attached to the CTD's underside facilitates a smooth descent in the water. Once the device reaches the bottom, we bring it back to the surface and then repeat the procedure. This time, on the way back down, we pause its descent twice for exactly a minute at equal intervals so it can better calibrate itself and collect more detailed information. All the data is stored in the device, but we routinely download it to a computer to ensure no information is lost. Depending on conditions, we try to take measurements twice daily. A boat the size of the *Arctic Joule* has drawbacks, but it has advantages too, including its ability to allow us to collect scientific data in a meaningful way that may help scientists better understand what's happening in Arctic waters.

The effect of climate change on our oceans is complex and open to much interpretation and debate, but climate change is clearly and fundamentally changing ocean properties in three distinct ways. The first is by altering ocean currents. Deep ocean currents are driven by differences in temperature and the salinity of seawater in a process known as *thermohaline circulation*. When sea ice forms, it expels salt into the surrounding water, increasing its density and making it sink. Warmer surface water is pulled in to replace the sinking water, where it too eventually becomes colder and saltier and sinks, creating a global oceanic conveyor belt. A decrease in sea ice affects thermohaline circulation, and an increase in fresh water born from the melting ice sheets affects it as well. This is happening in the waters around Greenland now. Scientific models postulate various outcomes—some catastrophic, others less so—but they all agree that a warming Arctic will alter thermohaline circulation with unknown consequences.

The second effect of climate change is that it's making our oceans more acidic. Each year, the oceans absorb about one-third of mankind's CO_2 emissions. This dissolved CO_2 creates carbonic acid (H_2CO_3), which reduces the ocean's pH level and makes it more acidic. The pH scale measures acidity with values ranging from 0 (most acidic) to 7 (neutral) to 14 (very basic). The historical pH norm for the ocean has been 8.17. Over the last two centuries this value has risen to 8.09, an alarming rate of change if one considers that over the last

300 million years the average pH of the ocean has not changed by more than 0.6 points. If CO_2 acidification continues to increase at this rate, scientists predict, pH levels may drop as much as 0.5 by the next century. The Arctic Ocean will experience the most dramatic impacts, as its colder waters naturally absorb more carbon. Diminishing sea ice will increase its exposure to the air, which will further accelerate absorption. A more acidic ocean will directly impact corals and shellfish, making it more difficult for them to build their skeletons and shells. A decline in coral and shellfish will decrease biodiversity and profoundly alter ocean productivity and biodiversity.[1] In short, a radical change in acidity in a marine ecosystem that's evolved in a stable pH environment for millions of years will have devastating impacts.

The third and most widely discussed impact of climate change will be rising sea levels. NASA satellite images have revealed that global sea levels have risen by 80 millimeters (over 3 inches) since 1992; in some parts of the world, they've risen as much as 250 millimeters.[2] A recent study found sea levels along the northeast coast of the United States had risen an unprecedented amount from 2009 to 2010, with the levels around New York City rising by 128 millimeters.[3] To those sitting on the fence about climate change, 128 millimeters—which is about 13 centimeters, or 4 inches—may not sound like much, but it's important to understand this is only the beginning, and mounting research suggests that the most widely accepted current predictions significantly underestimate the scale of what's to come.

A groundbreaking study by James Hansen, the former NASA scientist who put global warming on the world's radar almost three decades ago, is now warning of a "sea level rise of several meters" before the end of the century.[4] Hansen's shocking projection far exceeds the IPCC estimate of one meter in the same time, but Hansen has unearthed evidence showing that the IPCC climate model underestimates the sensitivity of the planet's ice sheets to warming and their contribution to sea-level rise. Two of the earth's largest ice sheets, in Greenland and Antarctica, hold 99 percent of the earth's fresh water as ice. If the entire Greenland ice sheet were to melt, it would mean a sea-level rise of over 6 meters; if the entire Antarctic ice sheet were to melt, it would mean a 60-meter sea-level rise. Even those who scoff at the impact of a 4-inch sea rise have to agree that the prospect of a 196-foot sea rise is scary.

This may seem alarmist to climate change deniers, but if Hansen's proven track record isn't enough to allay their skepticism, his research should be. His remarkable study in the peer-reviewed journal *Atmospheric Chemistry and Physics* uses a more advanced climate model that incorporates ancient paleoclimatic data combined with new satellite information to demonstrate that ice sheets can melt at a "non-linear" rate, releasing huge amounts of water in decades rather than millennia. Current observations indicate that certain ice sheets are already doing this.[5] For example, according to a recent study published in the journal *Science,* the Zachariae Isstrom glacier in northeast Greenland has entered a "phase of accelerated retreat" and is shedding mass at a rate of 5 billion tons per year. "The top of the glacier is melting away as a result of decades of steadily increasing air temperatures," says the study's senior author, Eric Rignot, "while its underside is compromised by currents carrying warmer ocean water, and the glacier is now breaking away into bits and pieces and retreating into deeper ground." The neighboring Nioghalvfjerdsfjorden glacier is also experiencing accelerated melting. If both disappeared, the global rise in sea level would be nearly a meter.[6]

According to the *Stern Review on the Economics of Climate Change,* commissioned by the British government, a one-meter rise in sea level by the end of the century—the most conservative estimate, and the one put forth by the IPCC— would jeopardize roughly $3 trillion worth of infrastructure worldwide—infrastructure that's critical for human civilization.[7] It would "drown some island nations such as the Maldives and Tuvalu," author Naomi Klein says in her book *This Changes Everything,* "and inundate many coastal areas from Ecuador and Brazil to the Netherlands to much of California and the northeastern United States, as well as huge swaths of South and Southeast Asia. Major cities likely in jeopardy include Boston, New York, greater Los Angeles, Vancouver, London, Mumbai, Hong Kong and Shanghai."[8] In other words, even a one-meter sea-level rise would be a catastrophic turn of events for our planet, yet James Hansen is predicting upward of a 3-meter rise unless greenhouse gas emissions are slashed. While climate change deniers warn of dire consequences to the global economy if we diminish our dependence on fossil fuels, the scientific evidence points to far more dire consequences if we don't.

WE CONTINUE ROWING for over thirty-six hours after leaving Paulatuk, passing around Cape Lyon on calm seas. Wikipedia defines *cape* as a "headland or a promontory of large size extending into a body of water, usually the sea [that] . . . usually represents a marked change in trend of the coastline";

for us, the definition should include "a marked change in for-tunes" as well. Cape Dalhousie, Cape Bathurst, and Cape Parry all represented serious challenges for us, as the weather and sea turned badly at the worst possible moment as we rounded each of them. But Cape Lyon is different. The 100-foot face, precipitous and blank, is nearly three miles long and in bad weather would be a very dangerous place, but the deep pulsat-ing rhythm of an ocean swell is the only thing marking our passage around it.

As we round Cape Lyon, we literally and figuratively turn a corner in our expedition. We're heading east now, with the big bays of Liverpool, Franklin, and Darnley behind us. Ahead lies a stretch of coast running roughly 280 miles east-southeast in a relatively direct line to Cape Krusenstern and the mouth of Coronation Gulf. The shore of Victoria Island, which now sits invisible some hundred miles to our port side, gradually shifts toward the mainland until it's a mere eighteen miles distant at Cape Krusenstern. About halfway along this shift, when Victoria Island is distinctly closer to the mainland, the body of water changes from the Amundsen Gulf to the Dolphin and Union Strait. At the eastern end of the Dolphin and Union Strait, just before the narrows at Cape Krusenstern, two small islands, called Lambert and Little Camping, respectively, sit between the mainland and Victoria Island to the north. They mark the end of the Dolphin and Union Strait, the start of the Coronation Gulf, and our crossing point to the southern shore of Victoria Island, the eighth largest island in the world.

The wind has been behaving extremely well for the last day and a half, other than throwing a three-hour temper tantrum as we approached Cape Lyon last night. Even so, we remain on edge, mistrustful, knowing it may turn at exactly the wrong moment. Like parents with a disruptive child, we've grown accustomed to our blustery bundle misbehaving when we don't want it to.

Out of Keats Point, a strong following sea—where the current is moving in the same direction we are—pushes us playfully for several hours. Near midnight, its mood seems to shift to anger, and we tuck into a small inlet to catch some sleep. By morning a thick bank of Arctic fog has replaced the wind and we pull anchor into a world of white blindness that evokes Nobel Prize winner José Saramago's *Blindness*, a harrowing novel of man's will to survive against all odds. Here in the fog, we're overwhelmed by a feeling of containment; the whiteness envelops us and plays tricks with our minds. It feels as if we're floating in the air, our sense of place shrinking away from the vastness of a world that has a horizon to one contained within a large bowl of milk. We can see nothing but the odd rolling wave that sweeps through our space to remind us that there is an ocean out there. It's a powerful metaphor for the Arctic: like the gentle oceanic swell born from far away moving through our bubble, the waves of climate change are perceptible here too.

By midmorning the fog has lifted to reveal a shoreline of cliffs and steep gravel beaches. There's little vegetation here, just rock and stone in myriad forms. In one dramatic flourish, a finger of rock extending out from land has collapsed to create an archway. The temptation is too great to ignore, so we alter our route and pass right through it.

We travel close to shore trying to spot wildlife, knowing full well the beaches are the prowling grounds of bears.

The polar bear's favorite food is the bearded seal, and we've seen many in recent days. The seals are inquisitive creatures who investigate us by swimming close to our boat, their whiskered faces just above the waterline and their large glassy eyes peering at us with wide astonishment. One bold creature swims directly beneath our hull on its back, gazing straight up at us as it glides by.

VIDEO DIARY, DAY 34

PAUL: We've had a good run of it over the last few days. We've been moving well ever since we left Paulatuk. Denis's beard is coming along nicely, too; it's quite ginger.

DENIS (*laughing*): I'm officially going to say that's a fucking beard, no matter who you are. Maria doesn't know what she's talking about—it's full beard ahead.

PAUL: Just to explain this now, Maria is an important member of the team that is doing stuff back home, and she made a comment when she saw a recent picture of us. It was like, "Oh, Denis seems like he's the only one who's shaving," and Denis has been quite sensitive about the beard ever since.

DENIS: Any sailor or Arctic explorer would be proud of that. (*He rubs his scruffy beard as he stares into the camera.*) A couple of weeks with this bad boy and I may just have to register it as a lethal weapon.

PAUL (*laughing*): There's a face there that only a mother could love, eh?

DENIS: Yeah ... *your* mother.

WE'VE BEEN NOTICING a certain consistency in the weather over the last couple of days, with the winds building in the evening only to subside again by morning. We needed to anchor for a few hours again last night before Frank and I started things off early today, as the sun came up. The orange glow of a sunrise lasts for hours this far north, and it's been especially pronounced in recent days.

After several hours of rowing, we stumble upon a decommissioned DEW Line station at Tysoe Point. We almost missed it, but the slopes of the shoreline look too perfect in both line and proportion to be natural. Huge berms of gravel extend for hundreds of feet, running parallel with the shore, and pipes randomly pop out of the surface. I can only imagine what nastiness is buried beneath to warrant such permanent venting. Two metal structures remain on site, one like a small airplane hangar with a large overhead door that is locked, and another that's a simple one-story shoebox. The main door has been ripped open from the underside and the interior ransacked, no doubt the work of a bear. A hundred yards away, a large block of concrete sits strangely disassociated from everything but bearing a plaque commemorating the site:

> From the mid 1950s until the early 1990s the PIN1 Clinton Point military radar station was located at this site. It was one in a series of military radar stations called the Distance Early Warning Line. Known as the DEW Line, it stretched across Alaska, Yukon Territory, Northwest Territories and Nunavut at this latitude. The North Warning System replaced the DEW Line in the early 1990s.

The inscription is written in English, French, and Inuktitut and displays the name "National Defence Canada" on it.

It's only a quick stop for us and we push off again into glassy seas bathed in the everlasting rosy morning light, but a windstorm soon brews up and we're on anchor again. This stop-and-go is becoming so familiar to us now that we've accepted it and perform it without complaint. The wind, which is coming from the south, is noticeably warmer, but there's something else different about it as well. It reminds me of the southerlies we experienced coming out of Paulatuk a few days ago, just a little stronger; there's also a distinct haze in the air, and I can even smell smoke.

For smoke to make itself felt in the passage means significant fires burning somewhere to the south. I didn't think I'd experience it up here, but a NASA satellite image shows a huge band of smoke running right across the southern part of the Northwest Territories; the haze from it extends throughout the region, explaining our prolonged sunrises.

The occurrence of wildfires farther and farther north is becoming the new reality in a warming Arctic. A 2013 study published in the *Proceedings of the National Academy of Sciences* found that the Boreal forest—the vast 600-mile-wide belt of birch, larch, and fir trees that stretches around the Arctic, separating the tundra of the North from the deciduous woodlands and temperate rainforest to the south—is burning at a rate unprecedented for at least the last 10,000 years. Extending throughout Russia, Europe, and North America, the Boreal forest accounts for 30 percent of the world's land-stored carbon, a mammoth, centuries-old reserve that will be released if the forest burns.

As we ride out today's windstorm, the Siberian region of the Arctic is getting hammered by wildfires. The summer of 2013 will prove to be the worst wildfire season Russia has experienced in over a decade. A huge high-pressure system is currently stalled over northern Russia and is driving temperatures to unprecedented levels. The Siberian city of Norilsk, where daytime highs are normally about 60 degrees Fahrenheit (16 Celsius) in the summer, is currently experiencing temperatures up to 90 degrees.[9] It's particularly disturbing that these fires are occurring some 560 miles farther north than they might normally be expected, spreading soot and ash throughout the Arctic region. Even the surface of Greenland's vast ice sheet has become darkened by ash; by the end of this summer, because of solar heat gain of the darker surface, 95 percent of its surface ice will have melted.[10]

The summer after our expedition will prove to be the worst wildfire season ever for the Northwest Territories. Huge fires, fueled by unseasonably hot and dry weather, will blanket Yellowknife, the Territories' capital city, with a thick haze of smoke and ash. Sections of Highway 3, the main artery into the city, will shut down, cutting off Yellowknife's 19,000 residents from the outside world. As the entire community is put on a health advisory, Dave Phillips, Canada's senior climatologist, will declare 2014 the driest summer the Northwest Territories has ever experienced. Climate models hadn't predicted this for another four decades,[11] which fuels concerns that forecasts from current models may be too conservative.

The tundra that sits between us and the tree line can burn too if the conditions become dry enough. In 2007 a lightning strike on Alaska's North Slope ignited a tundra fire that burned for three months until October snowfalls extinguished it. The fire expanded to over four hundred square miles in area, the largest fire to hit the region since recording began in the 1950s. The charred scar on the landscape is big enough to be visible from space. A 2011 study in *Nature* found that the 2007 fire sent as much carbon into the atmosphere as the entire Arctic tundra stores in a year.[12]

VIDEO DIARY, DAY 36

DENIS: The wind is coming straight against us. The weather up here is so bizarre, we have this very strong wind right in our face but it's like a desert wind, it's super warm, crazy.

THE SHARP SNAPPING of the flags on our boat—we have two of them, one Canadian and one Irish, suspended from the antenna by our cabin door—sound like whips snapping in the air and indicate a very strong wind, likely gusting over thirty-five knots. We notice on our navigation screen that we're moving; the wind is pushing the *Arctic Joule* so hard that we're dragging our anchor across the ocean floor and we're forced to deploy our backup anchor to stop ourselves. It's disturbing to think that our single anchor can't resist this wind, and a relief when the second one works, holding us fast until the wind dies.

Frank and I begin rowing in earnest again in the calm, but we don't realize our windstorm is only taking a deeper, more powerful breath before it unloads its full fury. Soon thundering gusts begin to strafe us and we're forced to stop again. We drop both anchors in anticipation of what's coming and head back into the cabin to wait it out.

"Fuck! This wind is crazy!" I say to Frank as I shut the hatch door behind me. "This is the strongest wind we've felt so far."

Denis is staring at the navigation screen mounted on the inside cabin wall. He looks alarmed. "We're moving out, guys. You should toss the second anchor."

"We already have," Frank says.

Denis taps the screen. "Look, you can see our line. We're being pushed straight out. This isn't good."

The onboard GPS, which traces our movement on the display screen, shows clearly that we're moving out to sea. It's just a few yards a minute, but we're moving nonetheless. The farther out we're pushed, the deeper the water gets. Our second anchor has only sixty feet of line before it loses purchase.

"If we lose that anchor," Frank says, "there'll be no stopping us. We're going straight out to the pack."

Sea ice still sits a short distance offshore; being pushed into it would be disastrous. Getting caught in the icy maelstrom outside the cabin is a nightmare none of us want to consider; our boat would likely be destroyed. Our depth gauge indicated 35 feet when we anchored a short time ago. We now watch the screen as that number increase like a rocket countdown in reverse, with 60 feet spelling catastrophe.

... 45 feet...

... 46 feet...

... 47 feet...

The wind has built into a furious gale, more powerful than anything we've experienced on this expedition; it must be gusting at over 40 knots. The boat is being tossed around like a cork and we're slipping fast.

... 48 feet...

... 49 feet...

... 50 feet...

We throw our sea anchor to slow the movement, but it's of

little help. Three anchors and we're still not holding ground. We're powerless against this push.

... 51 feet...

... 52 feet...

... 53 feet...

Sometimes in adventures, at moments like this, the only thing separating a good outcome from a really bad one is blind luck. Today we're served a heaping scoop of it.

"It's stopped," Paul says, scrambling out on deck with a flummoxed look on his face. "It's crazy-like."

The wind has completely stopped, as if someone flipped a switch off.

"Christ, let's get to shore before it starts again!" I scream.

Paul and Denis jump into the rowing stations while Frank and I haul the two ground anchors as fast as we can. I scramble off the bow and retrieve the sea anchor.

"We're good, guys," I yell to Paul and Denis when the sea anchor is out of the water. "Go, go, *go!*"

They haven't rowed more than fifty strokes before the wind switch is flipped back on.

"Fuck!" I scream. "You're looking great, guys! Keep it going, keep it going!"

Paul and Denis row like men possessed.

"We can do this, guys. Keep it going, guys. You're looking great."

I'm their eyes now, squeezed between them on deck, manning the steering wheel and ensuring we hold a straight line. In a strong wind like this, the bow wants to slip to one side or the other and throw the boat broadside. Someone has to steer constantly, which a rower can't do without stopping rowing.

"One hundred meters to go, guys," I lie, encouraging them to pull harder than I think they can. They can't see where the shore is, and we're still a lot farther out than I tell them, but they're fighting this thing through ... somehow.

Weeks of hard rowing are paying off. Paul and Denis are keeping the tempo up, showing no sign of tiring. We claw ever closer to shore.

"Seventy-five meters out, guys, seventy-five meters out!" I scream truthfully now. "Go, go, go. You're making Crean proud."

Tom Crean was a heroic Irish polar explorer and member of both Scott's and Shackleton's Antarctic expeditions. He was one of the crew rowing the twenty-two-foot *James Caird* on the eight-hundred-mile journey from Elephant Island to South Georgia in April 1916, one of the greatest ocean-boat journeys of all time. We have a book on board detailing his exploits. The boys know his story well.

A large swell pushes the *Arctic Joule* up hard onto the rocky beach.

"I don't know how you guys did it, but you did it!" I scream, hitting them both hard on their shoulders as I leap off the boat. "You guys are fucking amazing!"

We immediately hit our battle stations, with Denis and I rigging an anchor high on the beach and Paul and Frank fighting to keep the *Arctic Joule* perpendicular to the waves. Standing in the surf manhandling a one-ton boat as the waves are tossing it about is a recipe for disaster, so after Denis and I secure the anchor, Frank and Paul let the *Arctic Joule* turn broadside to the waves and wash up onto shore.

The wind intensifies to a level I can't even guess at. The gusts are so powerful that beach sand is lifted into a sandstorm.

Paul and I attempt to set up our tent, a model designed for these conditions, but within minutes a gust flattens it, bending one pole horribly and snapping another altogether.

We spend the rest of the evening watching helplessly as the wind bashes the boat about in the large surf. By 4:30 a.m. August 9, twenty-four hours after starting our day, the storm has finally begun to subside. Paul and Denis slip into the cabin to get some sleep while Frank and I set up our sleeping bags onshore to keep an eye on the anchor. It's an odd scene, an endless gravel beach stretching into the dusk, two red sleeping bags in a straight line, foot to foot.

"We can both grab the gun here easily enough," Frank says, slipping the shotgun between our feet. Beaches are the pathways for bears, after all. "Just sit up and—boom," he says.

We fall asleep to the buzz of mosquitos, a strangely pleasant replacement for the sound of the wind in this bleak and hostile world.

THE POWERFUL SOUTHERLY eventually disappears, and we push the *Arctic Joule* off the gravel beach to resume our steady grind east. Frank and I hug the shoreline and I stare out across a landscape of uninterrupted rock. There's no green speckling its surface anymore, just an endless canvas of gray awaiting the return of the annual wash of white.

My temperate sensibilities first perceived the Arctic as a vast and untenable place, a barren land without life. But on this long journey, as my eyes have begun to linger on the landscape, I've come to notice life looking back at me. Sometimes it's the piercing stare of a snowy owl; other times, the playful splash of a bearded seal. Still other times, life explodes in the form of the crazed gallop of a young caribou running frantically down a beach, its head swinging wildly, or an unexpected blast of moist air erupting from a behemoth gliding through the water below us. Life here is elusive: a river mouth that appears barren until it's teeming with arctic char, a lagoon that's placid and empty until hundreds of beluga speckle its waters white. Life here is different, and I've needed to change my pace and perspective to fully appreciate it.

We manage another day of reasonable travel until our southerly wind builds again. It's two in the morning on August 10, and Denis and Paul are fighting into shallower waters.

"Lads, check it out!" Paul yells. "I think there's a light out there."

Frank and I poke our heads out of the cabin. There's a bright light out on the western horizon, and it's quickly growing in intensity.

"You think it's the Coast Guard?" Denis asks as he and Paul start to pull on their PFDs. Maritime regulations require access to PFDs but not that we wear them at all times. I often wear mine over my Ocean Rodeo dry suit just to keep warm. But Paul's and Denis's instinct to don their PFDs reflects the uncertainty we're all feeling. If it's the Coast Guard, we want to look like we're fully in control, even if we're not.

"Christ, I hope we didn't accidentally turn on our EPIRB!" I say. An emergency position-indicating radio beacon alerts search-and-rescue services by transmitting a coded message via satellite and earth stations to the nearest rescue authorities. Turning one on by accident would be a monumental mistake that would involve boats or planes coming to our rescue.

"We couldn't have, though," I say. "The case is closed."

The EPIRB is located on the starboard side of the head wall of the bow cabin. It's protected by a hard plastic cover with a large yellow latch that needs to be engaged to expose the unit. It's untouched.

It's also possible that our SPOT Satellite GPS Messenger is transmitting. The SPOT allows us to relay our location back to a tracking map on our website. It also has a 911 function that will send a message to rescue authorities if engaged. We turn the device on and off routinely to save the batteries; an accidental employment of its emergency function is not beyond possibility. I slide inside the cabin to check it out, and find that it's turned off and not transmitting. "It's not that either," I yell from inside the cabin.

When I return to deck the single light has morphed into four, all moving independently of one another. "What the hell is it?" Paul asks of no one in particular.

A growling noise cuts through the wind. The evenings are getting much darker now and our ambient light is like at sunset, when the sun has dipped well below the horizon, yet a band of orange still keeps the inky blankness of night at bay. The lights build in intensity, as does the snarl emanating from them. We can't see a thing until they're completely on top of us.

A pod of four Jet Skis and their support boat surround us. It's a surreal moment as camera lights from the support boat blind us and the roar of their engines make conversation difficult. We learn they're an American team filming a series for the television program *Dangerous Waters*. They started in Inuvik, as we did, and hope to make it through the Passage and, unbelievably, on to London, England, before year-end.

Jet Skis can travel at speeds upward of sixty miles per hour while we're struggling to maintain one. "They're going to be through the passage in days," I say in disbelief as they tear off into the night. It's just minutes before they're out of sight, the faint smell of petrol the only hint they were ever here.

It's not long before we're on anchor again, the wind too strong to row against. The sea floor is rocky here and is providing excellent purchase for our faux anchors. The two anchors we salvaged in Paulatuk last week aren't true anchors but reasonable facsimiles; one is a three-fingered hook that once acted as a buoy anchor, and the other is simply two pieces of $1/2$-inch plate steel (roughly an iPad in length and width) welded together by a $1/4$-inch diameter steel bar. In a sandy seabed like we experienced, they tend to slip, especially when it's been blowing as hard as it has been.

Fortunately, they don't slip today. We're stuck on anchor for thirty-six hours. On the afternoon of August 12, the wind finally begins to ease up. It should help us relax, but we're starting to feel pressure to achieve the goal we've set for ourselves. Although the air is still warm, we know by the evening darkness that winter is fast approaching. From this point forward, there's ten fewer minutes of light every day, and traveling in the dark ramps the danger meter up even higher.

THE BEACHES OF the Northwest Passage catch the detritus of the Arctic waters, leaving it on display for all to see. Rusty oil drums rank as the hands-down leader in Arctic rubbish, their matte reddish tinge regularly catching our eyes against the steely gray background of rock and stone. The sheer number of used drums speaks to the difficulty of motorized travel in the region, as does their abandonment on the landscape.

Driftwood abounds on the beaches, the massive outflow of the Mackenzie River still felt as far afield as the Dolphin and Union Strait, where we are now. (We passed out of the Northwest Territories into the territory of Nunavut about twelve miles after the Clinton Point DEW Line station and entered the Dolphin and Union Strait about forty to fifty miles after that.) The abundance of driftwood makes for a ready supply of firewood when we need it. Styrofoam is common here as well, its properties resisting decomposition like few other materials.

The other day we stumbled upon a strange device that looked like something from outer space. A stainless-steel cage encircled six plastic flotation balloons and housed a long blue and white instrument with three orange-faced saucers at its end. I'd never seen anything like it before. We marked the point with our GPS and took down the company information posted on it. I sent them an email to let them know where the device lies and received a reply from the company today: "What you have found is a device that measures ocean currents. Before breaking free of its mooring it has been deployed about 100m below the surface, measuring current speed and direction for every five meters of the water column. Data from these sensors are used by scientists to map ocean currents around the world, in order to understand our environment better." It's fascinating to think such things are out here monitoring and measuring. The company thanks us profusely for the information and says they will attempt to collect the expensive device as soon as they can.

FOR CENTURIES THE rock-strewn ramparts of the Northwest Passage have borne witness to great loss. Frank and I are gliding across mirror-flat waters in a charcoal twilight when we spot a large dark object on the otherwise flat gravel beach. As we move closer to shore to get a better view, the unmistakable profile of a ship's hull takes shape. It is situated twenty to thirty yards up the bank and sits upright, its starboard side running parallel to the beach. Paul and Denis are asleep in the cabin. The air is perfectly still. Frank and I nudge the *Arctic Joule* into the shallows and jump ashore. I anchor us to the beach by tossing the anchor onto the gravel. There's no fear of her going anywhere here.

The shipwreck sits virtually intact, its final moments perfectly on display. Faint bands of red and white give way to the weathered gray boards of the hull; indistinct letters on the bow seem to spell out RERUDE-B. The boat is roughly sixty-five feet in length and rises to a height of ten feet at the bow. An aft cabin, almost a perfect cube, sits at the stern of the boat. A large opening on deck has no hatch and reveals a dark, empty hull. A boat of indeterminate age, stranded alone, history unknown.

Within twenty-four hours we spy another shipwreck onshore, fully intact; this one is a much bigger boat with rusted steel throughout and masts still standing at attention. She too lies parallel to shore, but her bigger hull sits right down at water's edge. Fans of jumbled limestone sweep upward behind her, and the detritus of a crumbling rock prow looms beyond.

THE LAST COUPLE of days have been tremendous for us, with the wind dying and our rowing efforts continuous. But all things come to an end, even good ones, and our southerlies return with a vengeance. The forecast includes twenty-five- to thirty-knot winds for the next couple days, so, thanks to sage advice from our meteorological eyes in the sky, we hunker down in a relatively protected bay at Cape Young. We've traveled over seventy-five miles in the last forty-eight hours, and our spirits are high as we head into our forced layover.

We've had steady correspondence with a retired meteorologist from northern Alberta named Patrick who reached out to us a few days back. He sent us an email questioning some weather-routing decisions we'd made and offered us his help for the rest of our journey. We've been relying on the weather forecasts from the Canadian Ice Service, as well as from Victor, our enigmatic weather router, but we haven't heard much from Victor of late and the Canadian Ice Service reports have proven to be extremely broad in their range and hopelessly inaccurate. We have nothing to lose by accepting Patrick's kind offer and quickly discover his forecasts are pinpoint accurate. He formulates them based on the information he collects from remote weather stations throughout the region. It doesn't take us long to dismiss the CIS reports altogether and totally trust our new guardian angel, whom we take to calling Pinpoint Patrick.

Our spirits are buoyed by the effort, and when morning brightens to a guarded calm, with Patrick forecasting a short lull, we jump at the opportunity. Remnants of DEW Line Site PIN-2 at Cape Young have been staring at us from our evening's moorage, so we pop in to take a look. These decommissioned sites feel far more desolate and lonely to me than the surrounding landscape, purely because of the echo of a past human presence. Poking around them is always eerie. This site is different than the others we've seen, boasting a grid of large metal shipping containers neatly placed in rows and columns, as cold and ordered as an accountant's ledger. A smaller stack of large plywood boxes on palettes sits adjacent to it. In an unhappy legacy to times past, a large sign boldly states, "CAUTION PCB STORAGE AREA TRESPASSING IS PROHIBITED." A gravel runway sweeps across the site, compact and usable. A large metal-clad airplane hangar lords over everything, its shape architecturally pleasing, with proportion and form reminiscent of postmodern expression. It's just all so strange in such a landscape.

WE STEAL SEVENTEEN miles on the day before a medium-force northwester builds, pushing us to our next point of protection. A thickening fog has begun to envelop us as well. Patrick suggests that the winds will intensify soon and they do, to near gale-force levels. Expedition travel is greatly aided by technology, with GPS, satellite phones, and navigation maps eliminating a significant amount of uncertainty and peril from adventure travel.

In 1826 John Richardson traveled these shores as part of Sir John Franklin's second overland expedition to find the Northwest Passage. Franklin and Richardson descended the Mackenzie River together in June 1826 and parted ways on July 4, when Franklin headed west toward Icy Cape in the Alaskan Territory (then under Russian control) and Richardson headed east toward the mouth of the Coppermine River, a site now called Kugluktuk. Richardson employed two large expedition canoes, the *Dolphin* and the *Union,* which had been specifically adapted for ocean travel; hence the name of this section of the passage. He abandoned the *Dolphin* and *Union* at Bloody Falls, so named for a massacre that occurred on Samuel Hearne's 1771 Coppermine expedition, when his Dene guides came upon an Inuit camp and killed all twenty men, women, and children. From Bloody Falls, situated at the mouth of the Coppermine River, Richardson returned overland to Fort Franklin on Great Bear Lake.

Together, Richardson and Franklin charted over 1,800 miles of new coastline along the Arctic coast and made such extensive natural discoveries that they required two books to record them. These waters were little more than an icy quagmire in Richardson and Franklin's time, and the thought of venturing across them without any of the technological luxuries we take for granted today is awe-inspiring. I'm sure they would have relished a Pinpoint Patrick in their arsenals.

We get to shore in a sheltered lee and, as I've been able to fix the poles that snapped when we tried to set up the tent in the windstorm the other night, we sleep in the tent rather than the cramped cabin of the *Arctic Joule*. The terrain here is flat and low-lying, with grassland, tidal flats, and gravel bars all wrestling each other for a meager share of dry ground.

"Check these babies out," Frank says during our search for a good tent spot. "They look pretty fresh, too." I walk over to take a look. The paw prints are a little over twice the size of man's hand, with divots from long claws radiating out from the pads. The paws turn inward in a slightly pigeon-toed stance—an unmistakable sign of a grizzly bear. The tracks look dug into the mud as if the creature had been running in an explosive gallop from something, maybe a strange object approaching through the fog. I wonder quietly how big a bear it would take to produce such a print, not realizing we'll soon find out.

10

ESCAPE TO
VICTORIA ISLAND

OUR PREVIOUS NIGHT'S STORM BLOWS itself out by the middle of the next afternoon, Friday, August 16, and we start moving again. The weather report is grim, but we hope to poke along and steal another couple of miles like we did yesterday. We make the first of two moderately large crossings through choppy water in light winds before the sea begins to build and we slip into a well-protected bay for dinner and some sleep.

By 12:30 a.m., it's dark and raining and we're in our sleeping bags ready for sleep. Night creeps up on us more quickly every day; in just over a month, darkness hours will match daylight hours. Last into the cabin, Paul observes that the wind has died. Windless conditions, no matter when they occur, mean movement for us, and it's Frank's and my turn at the oars.

"Pop in a quick three-hour session?" Frank quips with little enthusiasm, curled up in his sleeping bag.

"Sounds good," I lie groggily. "Let's do it."

Moments like these reveal the difficulty of this expedition. There's no downtime out here, just moments of acting or waiting to act. We slip on our dry suits and shuffle out on deck.

"Good on ya, boys," Paul says with a laugh. "We'll see you in three."

We slip out of our bay with a bruise of clouds pushing across the horizon and a misty drizzle dropping a wet blanket on us. I slip on my earbuds under my hood and try to lose myself in the twilight and Pink Floyd—pain receding, becoming comfortably numb.

Frank and I finish our shift, and Paul and Denis have made it about halfway through theirs when a strong current stops us. We're anchored about three hundred feet offshore in very shallow water with Denis sitting at the oars when he spots our grizzly. "I see a bear," he states matter-of-factly. "No, really. I see a brown bear."

He's lying in the kelp at the edge of shore, oblivious to us. But he's a giant, with massive shoulders supporting a huge dish-faced head and a distinctive hump on his back. He's unmistakably a grizzly bear.

Frank slips out of the boat to get a steady shot with the video camera—the boat is rocking and the water is only a couple of feet deep, even this far out. He's quiet, but not quiet enough. The bear notices us, rears up on his hind legs, and starts shaking his head back and forth, seeking our scent. Aware of us now, he's not afraid—far from it. He starts moving toward us in the water, his body language speaking to us on a primordial level. His head is low and the hair on his back seems to be standing erect. He moves slowly, deliberately, eyes locked on us, his body language saying it all. On some primitive level, this bear has tapped into our vestigial fear of being hunted. Denis grabs the shotgun and readies for a shot into the air, but our bear is just letting us know who's the boss. After a few minutes he turns and slowly heads back to the kelp, where he sets about making a bed much like a dog would and lies down to rest. When he finally lowers his head, he turns it away from us, disinterested and unafraid. We've just experienced a moment we've been awaiting for the whole trip.

UNTIL TWO DECADES ago, grizzly sightings in the High Arctic were so rare that biologists considered any evidence of one a biological anomaly—more likely a bear lost for some unfortunate reason than a harbinger of things to come. But no more.

In 2003 Canadian glaciologist John England observed a grizzly bear along a river valley on Melville Island over 700 miles farther north than biologists would expect to find it. England described it as fat, healthy, and perfectly comfortable in its surroundings. "The clear implication was that this grizzly had denned somewhere up around Melville, far from where grizzly bears are normally found," England says in an article in the magazine of the National Wildlife Federation. "Presumably, it was feeding on muskoxen because apart from the occasional caribou you see high up on the Arctic islands there isn't much else for them to eat."[1]

Biologists surmise that these grizzlies are following caribou on their annual migration from the mainland to the islands of the archipelago and, with rapidly melting sea ice breaking up behind them, are finding themselves stranded farther north than ever before. But instead of struggling in their new environment, it would appear, some of them are adapting by eating seals, hibernating, and even interbreeding with polar bears.

The very idea of a polar bear and a grizzly interbreeding seems fanciful, but it appears to be a new reality. Polar bears diverged from grizzly bears about 5 million years ago[2] yet still maintain enough genetic alignment to produce fertile young. Biologists have observed such interbreeding in captive bears, but the existence of a naturally occurring mixed bear was considered hypothetical until April 16, 2006, when hunter Jim Martell shot what he thought was a polar bear near Sachs Harbour on Banks Island, N.W.T. The bear had a creamy white coat like a polar bear but long claws, a shallow face, and a humped back like a grizzly. It even had brown patches around its eyes and on its nose, back, and one foot. Martell was understandably distressed, as unlawfully shooting a grizzly bear in Canada can carry a $1,000 fine and up to a year in jail, but when the authorities were brought in, DNA tests proved the animal had a polar bear mother and a grizzly father, exonerating Martell and giving him the dubious distinction of killing the first grizzly–polar bear found in the wild.

On April 8, 2010, David Kuptana, an Inuvialuit hunter, shot what he thought was a polar bear until DNA tests proved otherwise. Not only was this bear a hybrid bear, it was a second-generation one, with a grizzly for a father and grizzly–polar bear hybrid for a mother.

With its presence transcending myth, the hybrid grizzly–polar bear has become subject to the name game. The amusing "pizzly" defines a bear with a polar father and a grizzly mother, while the equally jovial "grolar" refers to the opposite. But despite the lighthearted names, there's nothing playful about this bear. "It's the meanest of the lot," Joe Illisiak said when we were at Brown's Harbour. "You don't want to run into one of them."

A barren-ground grizzly bear is terrestrial and territorial, while a polar bear is nautical and nomadic. A grizzly bear's diet ranges from berries and roots to ground squirrels and caribou, while polar bears eat seals exclusively. Grizzlies are shaggy and brown, well camouflaged in the tundra, while polar bears are creamy white and well camouflaged on the ice. Mix a polar bear and a grizzly bear together and you get a hybrid species not well suited to either of its parents' worlds.

With Arctic warming, barren-ground grizzlies are venturing farther north than ever before while shrinking sea-ice habitat is forcing polar bears onto land. As the overlap between the two species' habitats increases, more pizzlies and grolars are inevitable. This new hybrid bear speaks loudly to the changes happening in the Arctic and to the threat facing the polar bear as a species. Scientists predict that two-thirds of the world's polar bears may disappear by the end of this century.[3]

This will be not only due to interbreeding but because they will be unable to adapt to food losses associated with a warming Arctic. According to a 2006 study in the journal *Science,* researchers attached satellite collars and surgically implanted small logging instruments on over two dozen polar bears in the Beaufort Sea in order to track the bears' movement and record physiological data. The results showed the bears didn't slow down when faced with a reduced food supply.[4] Scientists had previously surmised that polar bears would enter a state of "walking hibernation" when Arctic warming diminished their food supply, but this new research suggests that they will simply starve.

"If you or I were to be food-limited for weeks on end we would look like the bears' data," John Whiteman, the paper's lead author, from the University of Wyoming, said. "We think this data ... points towards their eventual decline."[5]

Canadian polar bear scientist Ian Stirling concurs with Whiteman. Stirling, who won the Weston Family Prize for Lifetime Achievement in Northern Research, has been studying and collecting data on polar bears for nearly fifty years and has observed firsthand the habitat changes for polar bears in western Hudson Bay. The polar bear population there is one of the densest in the world but consistently faces earlier spring sea-ice breakup each year. Since polar bears depend on sea ice to hunt seals, earlier breakups mean a shorter hunting season for them as well as for human hunters. "It's over three weeks earlier than it was only 30 years ago," Stirling says about the annual spring ice breakup he's witnessed. "That is just a phenomenal rapid change." If the Arctic continues to warm as projections indicate, Stirling predicts about half the polar bear population will disappear in the coming decades.[6]

THE STRONG CURRENT that stopped us earlier seems to have eased, and we decide to give it another go. We pull up our anchor and the clanging of metal against hull startles the beast still resting in the kelp bed. The massive bruin, standing well over 10 feet in height and weighing more than 1,100 pounds, takes off like a shot, moving with the grace and ease of a racehorse as he charges up the rocky beach. He slows only when he reaches the high point of the bank, giving us a cursory look over his shoulder and disappearing over the rise.

One of the challenges of traveling the Northwest Passage lies in trying to anticipate the impact of currents on our movement. The difference between a current with us and one against us is the difference between easy rowing and complete lack of forward progress. A strong current sweeping around the tip of Cape Bexley has held us in place for the last few hours. Although we've heard that the general background current in this section of the Northwest Passage flows from west to east, we've learned that site-specific factors like tide and wind play more important roles in predicting the impact of currents on our movement.

Before heading out on this expedition, I had a discussion with oceanographer Bill Williams at the Department of Fisheries and Oceans. The man behind our CTD testing operation, Bill cautioned me about the currents that form around Cape Bathurst on the Beaufort Sea. "When the wind blows from the west, you'll have a 4 kn current moving with you," he advised, "but an easterly wind will do the opposite." In the end, we really felt the current around Cape Bathurst after we rounded it and were swept south into Franklin Bay. We've found now that the wind and tide profoundly influence currents throughout the passage. The ebb and flow of tidal movement mixed with the push from the wind makes predicting currents something more akin to soothsaying than critical analysis. We find ourselves continually fooled by what we think should be the correct direction but isn't.

We start rowing again but quickly discover our current hasn't fully subsided. Even with only a light wind, we struggle to maintain a speed of two kilometers per hour, just over a mile per hour. With each oar stroke, we feel ourselves pulling the full weight of the boat—none of it is being pushed by the wind or the current—and we know we're fighting a losing battle. We row until our exhaustion trumps our frustration, and after a couple of hours we try again. This time we maintain a speed of 3.8 kmh, almost double our previous speed, with much less effort as the tide turns from ebb to flow.

Patience is one of the most important qualities an Arctic traveler can possess, and eventually it pays off. Over the next two and a half days we row almost nonstop in a steady succession of three-hour shifts, taking only three short breaks: a lunch stop of tea and chocolate, a short rest when the current picks up, and a quick trip into shore to investigate something strange. Frank spots it at the end of our shift. It looks like all the other big boulders dotting the shoreline until it moves. "Pass me the binocs, would you?" he says, looking intently at the mainland. "It's a muskox! You want to head in and check it out?"

We direct the *Arctic Joule* toward shore and start moving as smoothly and quietly as possible to avoid spooking our unsuspecting prey. It spots us, of course—we're a glowing white object set against a monolithic canvas of blue and gray, the only visual anomaly in this flat, featureless environment— and scampers off over the rise. It's likely a lone bull, drifting solo in summer months, until it finds a herd to travel with in winter. We anchor the *Arctic Joule* just offshore, wade through a few yards of knee-deep ice water to reach the beach, and trek inland in hope of catching a better look. The terrain is a mix of rock and tundra gently rolling off in all directions. It's not the ideal terrain to hide from pursuers, but our muskox seems to have done it.

"He couldn't have got very far," I say. "Where's he hiding?"

We make our way over a small rise that leads back down toward the water and there, lying on a rug of olive green tundra, is our quarry.

"Shhh. Let's move in easy and not scare him," Frank says. "He doesn't seem too bothered." We move carefully forward, knowing that the closer we get, the cleaner a shot we can take. My weapon is a Nikon D600, Frank's a Canon HV30.

The muskox rises to its feet when we're just over 150 feet away. His head is high and he's agitated. Frank keeps moving forward to within 100 feet, drops to a knee, and starts filming. The bull ramps up his threat display by lowering his head and rubbing it against the inside of his foreleg. This unique muskoxen behavior is called "whetting of the horns." He's rubbing a pear-shaped gland below his eye, which means he's pissed off. If he starts to tilt his head provocatively or rake his horns against the ground, we'll be running for cover. The boys have followed us out, and Denis readies the shotgun to fire a warning shot into the air if needed.

A muskox is a wild-looking creature. Large, bulging eyes protrude from its skull, clearing a way through the thick pelt to permit a wider view and conveying an almost crazed air. A frontal gown of long guard hair gives the beast the striking presence of a creature on the fringe, a barren-land shaman, an Arctic pirate. They remind me of the Rolling Stones' guitarist, Keith Richards, whose look is deliberately that of a pirate—so much so that Johnny Depp copied it when creating the character of Jack Sparrow for the *Pirates of the Caribbean* movies. When Richards passes, I could see him coming back as a muskox.

Although it looks like a cousin to the bison, the muskox is actually one of the two largest and stockiest members of the sheep/goat family, the other, its sole living close relative, being the takin of northern Tibet. It's also one of only a few large animals in North America to have survived the last ice age;

most of its ancestral companions, such as the mammoth, the short-faced bear, the dire wolf, and the North American camel, went extinct.

The Inuit call the muskox *oomingmaq,* meaning "animal with skinlike beard." Paul and I have respectable beards at the moment and even Denis looks like he's developing one, but Frank's is truly extraordinary. Its thickness and volume make it look like the product of years of neglect, though it's the same age as ours, so we have an *oomingmaq* on our team too: Frank, the "man with skinlike beard."

Within minutes of sighting him, Denis has named our muskox Murray. After a short time, our presence becomes too much for him—Murray, that is, not Denis. He turns away from us slowly, then explodes into a run, disappearing over a rocky ridge, left again to his lonely wanderings.

As we wade back to the boat I notice how much weight Denis has lost. His body is much slimmer than when we started; he now more closely resembles a track runner than a rugby player. Paul is slimmer as well, and Frank looks downright gaunt. Even through his forest of a beard you can see the sharp indentation of his cheekbones. I've been losing a lot too. We're all shedding the pounds like crazy. Inevitably, the topic of food is coming up more and more.

VIDEO DIARY, DAY 44

DENIS: We're kinda hungry. We're constantly talking about food.

PAUL: We're thinking about home, but you gotta be careful you don't wish away the trip as well 'cause you kinda take for granted and forget where you are—in the Arctic.

DENIS: Paul has a little song that he's prepared for us so. It's called, "Lindsey, I Love You."

(*Paul says nothing but shakes his head.*)

DENIS: We talked the other day about what nickname he's going to give Lindsey. He's going to call her Pop-Tart.

PAUL: On the subject of Pop-Tarts, we temporarily misplaced the Pop-Tarts on the boat... and in fairness, Den-Den found them in the hatch and now we have Pop-Tarts again, so I do like eating Pop-Tarts.

DENIS: Pop-Tarts are essentially to us like cigarettes would be in prison. The currency is Pop-Tarts. Who would have guessed that Pop-Tarts are the bomb?

THE CROSSING FROM the mainland to Victoria Island is a hurdle we've been anticipating for some time. We begin our traverse at the narrowing of the Dolphin and Union Strait where it feeds into the Coronation Gulf, and we plan to use Lambert and Little Camping islands, which sit in the middle of the strait, as points of protection if inclement weather rolls in.

The narrowing of any large body of water always increases currents and ocean anomalies, and we're concerned about that now. In so many ways, we're like a cork in these waters, going where the wind and currents take us. We counter it by anchoring when we can or trying to anticipate where we'd be pushed if we can't, but sometimes, like when we rounded Cape Parry and were pushed toward the pack ice in Darnley Bay, it's out of our control. In that instance, we'd done everything we could yet were nearly cast into a heaving mass of ice akin to a thousand steel shipping containers grinding together. It was a sobering moment that said much about this expedition—you can plan all you want, but when you're trying something new you will always encounter the unanticipated. In the last fifteen years, I've climbed active volcanoes in Java, followed jungle patrollers hunting poachers and illegal loggers in Aceh, been caught in a raging ground blizzard on the Bering Sea coast of Alaska, crossed bottomless crevasses atop crumbling snow bridges in Antarctica, narrowly avoided deadly snakes, and been on the wrong side of a jihad and the wrong end of a gun. But through it all, I can honestly say nothing has compared to this expedition for its utter lack of control and potential danger.

On our crossing, we cut the corner from Camping Island to Victoria Island, heading straight across Austin Bay to Lady Franklin Point. The exposure to weather is more daunting on this line, but the time and distance we'll save are impossible to resist. Fortunately, the weather doesn't deteriorate until the final minutes of the crossing, and we pull into another DEW Line station at the tip of Lady Franklin Point.

There's a small shelter cabin onshore, and we're almost giddy anticipating a night in something other than our boat or tent. As the winds build and the skies darken, we unload the *Arctic Joule* and make our way to our evening shelter. Leaving the mainland and arriving on the shores of Victoria Island at the edge of the Coronation Gulf represents a milestone for us.

It's the evening of Monday, August 19, and we've finally found a little Lady Luck on a point of land named for Jane Griffin, far better known as the wife of the enigmatic explorer Sir John Franklin. Lady Franklin was the exact opposite of her bland, humorless husband, and she channeled her own go-getting personality into the stagnancy and lassitude of his. She was the driving force behind the stodgy Franklin, a dynamic and spirited woman overflowing with aspirations but hamstrung by the traditional Victorian values of her time. She pushed and challenged her husband, convincing him to head north and undertake his Northwest Passage expedition by arguing that the journey was essential for both his stature and his career. She has been quoted as writing to him, "The character and position you possess in society and the interest—I may say, celebrity—attached to your name, belong to the expeditions, and would never have been acquired by the career you have run, however fair and creditable, in the ordinary line of your profession."[7]

Lady Franklin was her husband's undying champion. When she realized his Northwest Passage expedition had likely met with disaster, she rallied the world to find him, sponsoring seven major expeditions in her search for information and stoically maintaining her search for his records even after it was known he'd perished. Lady Franklin never gave up on her husband or his legacy. Her seventh and final personally funded expedition left England in June 1875, a month before her death and a full three decades after Sir John had left her side.

WE HUNKER DOWN for the night in the small plywood-clad shelter. Muskox, caribou, and fox skeletons are scattered among the rocks along with various drying racks and tools used in the skinning process. This is obviously a hunting cabin, and from the sheer quantity of animal remains I'd say there's good hunting here, but it's also the perfect respite for us after several days of nonstop rowing. It's a guilt-free pleasure, too, as unfavorable winds are blowing outside. Spartan by normal standards, this thirteen-by-thirteen-foot box is like a five-star hotel for us. Plywood bunks and a cooking counter round out the interior and provide everything we need. Sleep comes easily.

An email from Victor greets us in the morning: "Congratulations on reaching Victoria Island. Austin Bay is always notorious for the bad currents and it is amazing you made it in the single shot. Lady Franklin Point and Becher Point are welcoming you."

Lady Franklin Point has welcomed us all right, but now she won't let us go. The winds have intensified overnight and we're here until they settle. Metal containers, domes, and structures from the decommissioned DEW Line station peer out at us over the shoulder of a gigantic artificial gravel ridge, beckoning to be explored. We've become aficionados of sorts of these Cold War–era relics. Paul joins me on the march up to the station. A cold wind is blowing, and we have our jacket hoods pulled up tight to keep the chill out. With heads down, locked in conversation, we nearly trip over the markers before we see them.

Protruding out of the gravel, just to the edge of our rocky path stand seven white crosses in a row, leaning and pitching like seven drunk men in a lineup. A slender mound of gravel extends out from each, speaking to something buried beneath. Remnants of older crosses lie scattered about, as does a bouquet of flowers some distance away, a few still holding their shape and color. It's a strange sight in such a lonely outpost. There are no markings on the crosses, and we're hundreds of miles from the nearest community. I can't help but wonder who these people were and what happened to them.

The DEW Line site is known as PIN-3 and remains a functioning part of the North Warning System, like the station we visited on Nicholson Island. The site is a by-now-familiar mix of satellite domes, metal towers, and long, low buildings, all housing for a world of machines. Human beings are unnecessary here; the site runs happily without them, chugging away with the cold, mechanical indifference of pure function. In many ways, these sites speak more to our inhumanity than anything else. They've spoiled this pristine landscape with the chemicals and fuels that have oozed from them and have fouled the Arctic with their presence. Built solely for military purposes, they make it clear there's no escaping man's negative actions. On January 10, 2000, this unmanned site caught fire and was almost totally destroyed; a side of me feels the fire didn't go far enough.

Paul and I don't spend long in this world of metallic detritus and quickly head back to the cabin. On our walk back to the shelter, we see three muskox trotting in single file across the horizon, their huge, hairy coats draped over four spindly legs that are all but hidden by the manes above. They look more like life-size puppets than live animals.

In our idle time, we shoot rounds from the shotguns to ensure they're still firing. Our gun-cleaning regimen of late has been sadly lacking, and we'd like to avoid a jammed gun in polar bear country. Frank finds an old piece of plywood and props it up with a few rocks as a target. The intensity of a shotgun blast always surprises me; the thump in the crook of my shoulder feels like a hard punch. Denis is keen and has a go himself.

"Jesus Christ, that's fucking powerful," he says, realizing he's missed the plywood completely. He unloads another three shots at the target and misses every one, telltale splashes exploding in the water offshore. "I don't know if I like guns," he says, handing it to Frank.

"Good thing there's nothing out on the water, with your aim," Frank jokes. He's looking out to the water as he says it, but it's the horizon that holds his gaze. "Wait a minute...," he says, his voice trailing off before coming back with, "What's that?" He points to a small dot on the horizon. It's a long way out, likely six miles or so—far out of shotgun range, thank God—but the longer we stare at it, the bigger it gets. It's coming our way.

It's not long before the small black blob morphs into a small white sailboat with a red sail and two sailors. One evening eight days ago, while riding out a southerly storm on anchor in the Dolphin and Union Strait, a boat slipped out of the dusk and pulled up beside us. It was only a day after our Jet Ski encounter, and we weren't expecting company. The sailboat was under motor and able to navigate the strong wind with ease. The two sailors on board eased off the throttle to remain motionless about thirty feet off our port side. It was a Swedish boat, a thirty-five-foot steel-hulled ketch called *Anna,* which had wintered near Nome, Alaska, the previous year and was now on its way through the Passage. The wind was too strong and the distance between our boats too large to speak for long, but we exchanged smiles and the camaraderie unique to fellow travelers in a remote environment. Just before departing, they mentioned that two Australians were on our tail. "I'd say they catch you by tonight," the Swedish skipper, Pelle Ivarsson, said. "They're moving at about six knots."

With our average speed at about 1.5 knots, we've been looking over our shoulder ever since, expecting these Aussies. Evidently, we've welcomed them with a shotgun salute. The small skiff glides past our point and slips behind us into the sheltered bay where we've anchored the *Arctic Joule.*

The boat arrives and out hops an easygoing Australian, a slim fellow with a thick brown beard. "Howdy, mate," he says. "The name's Cameron, Cameron Webb." He's fully kitted in a dry suit with PFD but he's still chilled. We can hear it in his voice.

"We have hot drinks brewing up for you guys in the cabin," Denis says. "You're looking blue."

The other sailor tosses Cameron the bowline and follows him up onto the beach. "Matt McFadyen. Nice to see other faces out here," he says with a laugh, extending his hand.

Cameron and Matt are attempting to sail and row their seventeen-foot skiff through the Northwest Passage from Inuvik to Pond Inlet. Their boat is smaller and lighter than ours and can be hauled up onto a beach with inflatable pontoons, but today they take the easier option and moor in the small protected bay where we are.

"You know, mate, we almost caught you the other day," Matt says. "We saw you on the horizon but the weather blew up and we lost you."

"Yeah, we knew you guys were just behind us," Paul says. "Those Swedish guys in the *Anna* told us. We expected you guys to come flying by at any time."

"We were sure you guys snubbed us," Matt says. "We even joked about passing right by here now... Bloody Canadians," he says, laughing again.

Paul guffaws loudly. "We're Irish, and if we saw you we would have stopped for sure. The company around here is getting a little stale of late."

Matt and Cameron unload their gear and start constructing their tents. Their boat is too small for an enclosed cabin, and they need to set up camp when they sleep.

"You guys are more than welcome to crash in the shelter cabin, you know," I say. "It's no bother. We can make space."

"Thanks, mate, but our tents are good," Cam says. "We'll be up for those hot drinks, though."

It's not long before all six of us are shoehorned in the cabin, sharing stories and laughing at the madness of our adventures in a jovial game of one-upmanship. They've been suctioned to a Mackenzie River mud flat for the better part of one day, overwhelmed by a following sea that nearly sank them, and almost crushed by sea ice as it surrounded them. They heard about our anchor-cutting incident when someone emailed them to turn back and save themselves. They've been experiencing exactly what we've been experiencing and are likely the only people on earth who really know what we're going through. We learn that Cam is an experienced expedition kayaker and a polar guide, and Matt an Antarctic sailor and a three-time North Pole skier. They're both seasoned adventurers, equally in awe of this environment's hostility. The evening chat is comfortable and relaxed, a group of like-minded individuals sharing a unique moment, happy to be in each other's company.

THE MORNING OF Wednesday, August 21, dawns with a favorable northwesterly promising to push us down the Coronation Gulf. It's our cue to pack up. Matt and Cam will take a rest day.

"See ya, guys," Matt says as we shake hands. "We'll be seeing you again soon, no doubt."

"In Cambridge Bay, for sure," I say. "If you can catch us, that is!" But it's a joke. I know, with good winds, they'll pass us in a heartbeat.

We row out into a twenty- to twenty-five-knot wind that has us flying down the coast. It's a bumpy ride as the northwesterly keeps pushing us away from shore, but by day's end we clock in an impressive, but hard-fought, forty-five miles. Even though we're aware that the Arctic winter is just around the corner, a sense of optimism creeps into our minds that maybe things are changing for the better.

The Inuit have a word: *ilira*. It has no equivalent in English. *Ilira* is the sensation you feel when you glide down the waters of Franklin Bay under a setting sun with sulfurous plumes of smoke erupting from the hillsides and a giant bowhead whale surfaces just yards away. *Ilira* is the feeling you get when you go to sleep at night facing a mirror-smooth ocean and awake to a cauldron of sea ice, churning and grinding in its place. *Ilira* is the sensation you experience when a ten-foot-tall barren-land grizzly bear stands on its hind legs, discovers you're there, and slowly walks toward you.

Ilira is the flush of fear that comes with awe. Perhaps we would have been feeling *ilira* on that late August morning if we'd had any idea what was coming.

11

ILIRA

THE SHORELINE OF VICTORIA ISLAND eases from the water and gently rises to form perfectly uninterrupted ridges that run to the horizon. It looks like an endless series of high-tide lines marching upward and backward in time, because that's what it is. During the last ice age, vast glaciers covered Victoria Island, pressing down on the land. Once the ice melted and the landmass was free of its titanic load, it began to rise in isostatic rebound, with shorelines becoming stranded at higher elevations at ever greater distances from the sea. These layered beaches represent geological history right before our eyes.

The concept of time is different in the Arctic. I heard a story about a traveler discovering whalebones high on the shores of a small island off Svalbard. The bones were fully intact and seemed to suggest a fairly recent demise, but the traveler was perplexed because the bones were so far from the waterline. How could such a large marine mammal be moved so far up shore, so far beyond any possible storm surge? He was amazed to learn that the bones were in fact thousands of years old and had been preserved all this time, the remnants of a different time, in a place that has a different sense of what time actually is.

Our route takes us through an inland channel between Victoria Island and the Edinburgh and Richardson island group. We're unsure at first if the inside line is the most advantageous for us and even toy with the idea of heading out around the island group, but we stay the course and are happy for it.

The landscape changes dramatically once we enter the channel. Craggy walls and a precipitous cliff replace Victoria Island's gentle green and brown slopes. The rock looks different, too—more like a granite or quartzite as it pushes up from the earth below, blocky and steep. The stunning backdrop draws in on us as the passage narrows. Rock combs rise out of the water, forming islets that march down the channel, looking like the backbone of some giant sea creature that had been diving to the depths and petrified in the moment.

The cloud and drizzle that's been following us for days begins to thin as streaks of sun pierce the haze and paint our rocky world with a golden wash. The wind is calm but the current is strong and we maintain a brisk pace with little effort. The Arctic is a shy and retiring companion with a predilection for moodiness, but when treated with patience and understanding, it will share everything. It's doing that right now.

I spy movement on the craggy shoreline at the eastern end of the Edinburgh and Richardson island group. It's hard to make out from our distance—we're about a ½ mile away—but as Frank and I row in closer to investigate, we see a grizzly bear prowling the banks. When it detects us, it clambers up the cliff with amazing grace and ease. We're downwind, so it can't make us out, but it's still very curious. It bounds upward a few strides only to stop, turn back, and search for the unidentified odor. It finally sits at the edge of a cliff looking flummoxed and staring blankly at us with no idea of what we are. It's much slimmer than the one we saw on the mainland, and its coat is a colorful mix of blond and brown with hints of red. Its forelegs are jet black to the elbow and look like riding boots with formidable claws, the length of human fingers, poking out at the toes. After a few minutes of head shaking and uncertainty, it appears to catch our scent, wheels around, and charges up the cliffside. It's out of sight within a minute.

TRAVEL HAS BECOME pleasant for us in recent days but, according to Pinpoint Patrick, things are about to change. We slip out of the Edinburgh and Richardson island group to sprint ahead of an incoming gale that promises to hit the region tonight or early tomorrow morning with thirty-five-knot winds and snow. We're looking for somewhere suitable to moor and set up camp.

We sail down the coast of Victoria Island on a strong southwesterly that pushes us faster than we can row. Simply by cranking the rudder away from land, we slip along at a comfortable three miles per hour in exactly the direction we want to go. It's a bizarre scenario. Rowing the *Arctic Joule* requires pointing the bow toward shore to counter the forward propulsion that pushes her away from land. But this produces an inconsistent movement that forces us to constantly correct course. We zigzag in a back-and-forth motion, which proves slower than doing absolutely nothing. It's as strange as it is magical; the Arctic is giving us a freebie, at least for the moment. Our joyride lasts about an hour until the wind swiftly changes, hinting at what's coming—our cue to find shelter.

The shoreline along this section of Victoria Island is uniform and exposed. There are no protected harbors like the one at Lady Franklin Point, so we settle on the best we can find—a small indent that may give a modicum of protection—and head in.

The beach is moderately steep, but we haul the *Arctic Joule* as high up on it as we can. There are no large boulders to anchor our pulley system so we fill our large packs with gravel and use them as dead weight to haul by. It's a stopgap solution, but it's all we can do. *The Arctic Joule* weighs over a ton and doesn't manhandle easily.

We unload the boat and set up camp. As the storm builds, the surf begins pounding the *Arctic Joule*. The wave action has pushed her broadside and she's now being heaved up onto shore. If the waves work the anchors loose, the wind will push her out to sea and carry her away in moments. We put ourselves on an around-the-clock monitoring vigil, peering out from the tent every few minutes, waiting for the wind to die.

It doesn't die. It builds.

Trying to fill the tense hours, Paul and Denis film an entry to the video diary with a bit of gallows humor:

VIDEO DIARY, DAY 50

PAUL: Pretty wild outside. We secured the boat to shore, and she is getting beaten around. We have one of the anchor lines coming right up to the tent.

DENIS: Yeah, we have various different anchor systems, and the last one goes around someone's wrist, so if the boat drifts off the shore, someone is getting dragged out of the tent.

The tent walls shake and shudder violently. Several strong gusts push the fabric right down upon us, the tentpoles giving way to the extreme force. The guy wires, as taut as cables, prevent the poles from breaking. Large stones hold down the perimeter of the fly and help keep our shelter pinned to the ground.

"Fuck, I hope the tent can withstand this," I shout as I buttress the tent poles with outstretched arms on the inside, holding the crisscrossed arches of the poles on either side to prevent them from collapsing under the force of the wind. "This is a shitload more powerful than the gale they forecast."

I've endured winds like this in a tent only twice before, while skiing to the South Pole in 2008–9 and when traversing Siberia's frozen Lake Baikal in 2010. Each time I remained awake through the ordeal, waiting for our tent to be destroyed. In both cases, the tents survived, which is why we're using a tent from the same manufacturer now—Norwegian tent-maker Helsport—and I'm hoping the same holds true here. But that's not a certainty. This past spring a skier attempting a traverse of Greenland's icecap lost his tent is a windstorm and died from exposure. The value of a bombproof tent can't be overstated.

An updated weather report arrives. "Storm warning in effect. Wind west 55 knots diminishing to northwest 45 near midnight and to northwest 30 Saturday morning. Periods of snow and periods of rain and blowing snow ending late overnight. Visibility 1 mile or less in blowing snow." Sustained

55-knot winds equate to just over 60 miles per hour, with gusts typically rising to 40 percent greater again. An 85-mile-per-hour gust is well into hurricane force.

We monitor the boat through the daylight hours, peeking our heads out of the tent periodically to make sure nothing has shifted. The evening hours prove more difficult. Nights are dark now, and checking on the boat requires one of us to go out into those hurricane-force winds to see what's transpiring down at the beach. We do it every fifteen minutes, breaking up our sleep time into two-hour blocks and playing hearts to determine who gets the shifts. It's like pulling straws, with the worst hand being the shortest straw. Paul has improved his game, leaving me with the 4:00 to 6:00 a.m. shift.

I nestle myself in the vestibule as the others sleep, the wind howling around me. Whenever I check on the *Arctic Joule,* I also check the tent's guy lines. When I'm not out in the wind, I have a steaming cup of soup in my lap, my journal in my hand, and my shotgun at my side. The weather may not be fit for humans tonight, but it wouldn't deter polar bears, which could easily be prowling the beach. A couple of months ago in this situation, I might have been overwhelmed by *ilira,* the flush of fear that so often comes with awe here in the Arctic; but at this point, it all feels strangely familiar.

THE MORNING OF Saturday, August 24, dawns cloudy and cold. The wind still strafes us—not as strongly as last night, but still gale force. *The Arctic Joule* has taken a terrible hammering. A layer of fine gravel covers the deck, and the rearview mirror on the rowing deck has been smashed. As a result of the wind's continually thrusting the boat up onto the beach, some of the hull paint has worn off, and two of the sealed deck hatches have been compromised and are filled with seawater. The boat is like an exhausted boxer midway through a fight, sitting in her corner, badly beaten, but stoically waiting for the next round. We wait with her, knowing the storm will end, but not knowing when.

AS THE WIND subsides, Frank and I venture out to explore. Muskox dot the hillsides, their numbers abundant in what must be an Arctic haven for them. A large river valley twists away from the ocean, creating a distinctive sinuous rift that cuts sharply into the landscape. The valley walls are a mix of steep tundra and crumbling bluff, which spill onto a bed of river rock below. Only a trickle of water meanders through. We follow the rim of the valley inland for an hour, slowly climbing to a bench that allows us to slip down to the river and a route back to the boat. Dwarf birch and willow, which look like they normally tussle for space on the exposed slopes of tundra, now seem to cower against each other from the wind. A red splash of lingonberry explodes against the brown and green scrub. Caribou bones are scattered everywhere. Bands of exposed rock reveal a greenish tinge, probably from copper, as they disintegrate on their airy perch. The community of Kugluktuk, formerly known as Coppermine, is only just over a hundred miles away.

We head back to the tent and settle in for our third night stormbound. The wind continues to hammer the tent fabric outside, but it seems to be lessening in force, and Pinpoint Patrick has forecast it to end by morning. Denis and Frank are swapping the iPad back and forth in a game of Tiger Woods golf while Paul scribbles in his journal by headlamp.

"Guys, we need to talk," I say, looking at my watch to check the date. "What are we going to do? It's Sunday, August 26, we're almost into September, and we're nowhere close to Pond Inlet. There's no way we're going to make it in the time we have left."

Everyone looks up. This conversation has been a long time coming, and has been spoken about obliquely for weeks. Frank and I have talked about it at length in the cabin, as the boys have too, I'm sure. Winter is just around the corner and we have very little time left before the ocean begins to freeze.

"Yeah, the weather is getting worse and the days are getting shorter," Paul says. "It's getting cold out too. I agree, there's no way." Paul looks toward Denis, who twists his head to the side and purses his lips a bit.

"I know, we've been talking about it, yeah, there's no way," he says, and pauses for a moment. "It doesn't bother me in the slightest, though ... There's not an inch farther we could have gone."

"We should call it in Cambridge Bay," Frank says. "It makes no sense to push on to Gjoa Haven."

Cambridge Bay is just under 100 miles away; Gjoa Haven on King William Island is another 280 miles.

"I agree," I say. "Crossing Victoria Strait would be super sketchy, and for what? We're still not going to make it across the Passage."

The crossing of Victoria Strait between Victoria Island and King William Island will likely be littered with sea ice pushed down from the perennial ice stream to the north. This is where Franklin's ships the *Erebus* and the *Terror* met their demise, and it's where Parks Canada is conducting their annual search to find them. Making it to Gjoa Haven is a possibility, but only a slim one. Attempting it would come at great risk—a risk that increasingly feels like it doesn't bear a worthy return.

"Yeah, Cambridge Bay," Paul says, expressing what we're all thinking—what we all obviously have been thinking without talking about it as a full team. "It's not worth taking the chance."

Denis nods in agreement. "Cambridge Bay it is," he says. "But what about all those anti-climate-change fuckers who are going to pounce on this? Those bastards are going to have a field day with this one."

"Yeah... yeah... I know," I say, equally upset by this thought. "But they're going to have a field day with it no matter what we do. We're not going to make it across the full Passage."

"You can't let them affect our decisions," Frank says. "Ignore them. They're not worth it."

We realize there's nothing those folk would like more than to goad us into making a bad decision and then watch us struggle. In this case it would mean pushing blindly into deteriorating conditions with a strong likelihood of failure and the resulting need for a rescue—or worse.

That decides it. Cambridge Bay will be our final port of call. And not just because continuing with our original plan would pose a serious risk to our well-being. We have a choice; our rescuers wouldn't. It's our job to make the responsible call now, before we put our own and others' lives at risk. Doing otherwise, especially just because we want to prove something to the online trolls whose comments have been dogging us for this whole trip, would be selfish.

"You know, this whole thing's been incredible," Denis says, nodding. "We've had such an amazing experience."

His words echo all of our sentiments and speak to a positive change in his view of the expedition as well. Denis is known as a guy who gets things done. He joined this journey wanting to prove he was up for the effort. In Paulatuk he saw our slow pace as some sort of failure—a disgrace, as he put it—even though he knew full well we were doing everything in our power to move as fast as we could. I believe he was seeing himself through others' eyes and wondering what they might think—worrying that others thought he just wasn't up to the task. The frustration he displayed caused discord among us, sapped our morale, and exposed his inexperience.

But his behavior has changed markedly in recent weeks, and he's back to his old self. The trip has been a trial by fire for him—for all of us—but I believe he sees now that the validity of the journey lies in the effort made rather than the goal achieved. None of us has anything to prove. We're the ones out here facing the challenges and dangers in this environment; we're the ones balancing on that fine line between boldness and madness; we're the ones trying to make a statement because we care about the world we live in.

We undertook this expedition to cross the Northwest Passage from Inuvik to Pond Inlet solely under human power in a single season to bring awareness to the profound effects that climate change is having on the Arctic. We're not going to make it across the Northwest Passage this year. There's a chance no boats will. We've heard that Bellot Strait is still locked in ice and a number of motorized vessels transiting from east to west are waiting patiently to pass through. It's been a difficult year for both weather and ice, and we've done what we can. Hopefully, it's enough. It will have to be. Pushing on blindly, knowing there's no hope, would be both reckless and foolhardy.

Ilira has become part of our daily lives out here. Its gentle flush of self-preserving fear has tempered the daily awe of our experience and guided us through this beautiful, hostile land.

Cambridge Bay will be our finish. And we'll finish with gratitude for the journey we've had, without regretting a moment of it.

WE ROW CONTINUOUSLY for the next thirty-six hours, with a moderate northwester pushing us obliquely down the coast. The lingering twilight that has guided us through the late-night hours is completely gone now, replaced by a thick black curtain, impenetrable and opaque. But tonight we're lucky. The Northern Lights have arrived, and they drift across the nothingness like an ephemeral mist caught in the rays of a midnight sun, speaking to the magic of this Arctic world.

Morning reveals a thin sheen of ice covering the *Arctic Joule* and a shoreline that has begun to freeze. My feet are cold and my hands numb. The effort of rowing isn't enough to keep me warm anymore. Winter is closing in.

"Does this coffee taste salty to you?" I ask Frank as I make up a morning brew at the end of our shift. Grabbing my cup, he and takes a swig and grimaces.

"That's saltwater," he says.

I test the water from the fresh water ballast containers. "It's salty. The desalinator must be on the fritz."

The intake valve is below the waterline and took a beating in the storm. The desalinator in the hull was flooded with sea-water as well.

"We'll need to find some fresh water onshore," Frank says. "We can't drink this."

We make good progress over the evening hours, getting far enough up the coast to start our traverse of Wellington Bay. The twenty-mile crossing is daunting, as all big crossings are, but we move swiftly with a light southwesterly pushing us from behind. It's only in the final four miles that the wind shifts enough that we have to struggle to shore.

We slip into a protected lee, anchor the boat, and wade into shore in search of fresh water. Cape Enterprise, the promontory we land on, reminds me of the rockscape of the Edinburgh and Richardson island group, where huge slabs of rock dotted with boulders step upward in giant benches. The rock is broken in places, with cracks dropping deeply into the earth, forming subterranean passageways below the surface.

"Looks like a perfect grizzly den," I say to Frank, half joking, as we explore one in our hunt for water. But then I slip the shotgun off my right shoulder and hold it tightly in my hand. "This really does feel like a grizzly den."

We find a marshy section of tundra just above the rock benches with water flowing gently between several small pools, surrounded by an edge of lush green. We fill up our pot and our four one-liter bottles and head back to the boat.

"You lads fancy a cuppa?" Paul asks as we climb back aboard. "Maybe some hearts and a little choco—"

A noise, faint but piercing, catches my ear. "Do you hear that?" I ask.

Paul cocks his head. "Yeah. Yeah, I do."

The noise grows louder and soon a large powerboat speeds around the far point of the cape, its bow sitting high out of the water. Adjusting its course, it banks right toward us. The two men at the helm, one large and one small, cut the engine as they reach us. The bow sinks into the water and pushes out a wave as it glides up beside us.

"We heard about you guys on the radio," the larger man shouts over the noise of the idling engine. "You're not too far from Cambridge Bay now, you know?"

"We're waiting out the weather," Denis shouts back. "The protection here is good."

"It's pretty rough around the corner there," the smaller man shouts, pointing back from where they came. "Can't imagine it in a boat like that."

We learn the men are heading to their fish camp in Wellington Bay, which is just up and around Cape Enterprise. They've set their nets and are hoping for a big haul of arctic char. The fishing is good at the moment, and they tell us the weather is forecast to subside in the coming hours. The motor roars back to life and they're gone again as quickly as they arrived, but we only have time for a cup of tea and several hands of hearts before the sound of their engine breaks the silence again. The boat barely slows to a slide and the smaller man hands Paul a plastic bag.

"Enjoy," he says with a smile as the boat tears off around the cape.

Paul's left holding six and a half pounds of fresh arctic char in his hand. "Fancy some dinner, lads?" he says with a grin, holding the bag high above his head. We've been on an exclusively dried-food diet since leaving Paulatuk almost a month ago, and can't believe our good luck.

"I'll cook it up," Frank says.

"I'll make some more tea," Paul says.

And so begins the feast: lightly seared arctic char, sprinkled with lemon pepper zest and a touch of cayenne, washed down with scalding cups of Barry's tea.

"I don't even eat fish," Denis says, "but this stuff is incredible. This is one of the best days of my life."

We eat until we're bursting and then we eat some more. It's nightfall before we're done. Our spirits rise as the wind dies and we push out on our final leg to Cambridge Bay. The night is cold and clear, and the Northern Lights again dance across the sky. Despite the light show, the darkness grows so complete that Frank and I nearly run aground on the low-lying Finlayson Islands.

VIDEO DIARY, DAY 54

PAUL: It's five in the morning and we're just getting up for our shift in a few minutes. This is tough.

DENIS: Only two hours' sleep, kinda nearly ready to be finished now. Like, that's tough. It's freezing, freezing cold outside. Gear is damp. Feet are cold. It's hard to imagine why you volunteered for this. There must be a positive. We volunteered for it so... but maybe there's none.

PAUL: The positive is that we'll be in Cambridge Bay soon, getting reacquainted with—

DENIS *(laughing)*: Reacquainted with your own mickey, I bet.

PAUL: No messing, there's been none of that on this trip. Kinda nearly borderline religious. Well, most of us have, but not everyone has been on the trip. Isn't that right, Denis?

DENIS: Involuntary doesn't count.

Despite the ribbing, life for four men on a small rowing boat is a testing affair even at the best of times. The quarters are cramped and privacy is nonexistent.

One evening at twilight, Paul exits the cabin from the rear hatch and steps onto the perforated metal gunwale running up the starboard side. I can see he's preparing to defecate. He holds onto the grab bar on top of the rear cabin with one hand, drops his pants with the other, and begins to squat. This is how we all do it—off the back of the boat. Frank, Denis, and I are able to squat low enough to disappear from the rowers' view, but for Paul, with his injured hip, this is impossible, and he's left fully exposed to us. I can't imagine that's ever a moment to look forward to, but today's effort goes memorably wrong. The wind is gusting from the stern and Paul's raised position allows a blast of foul air to find its way directly to me. Rowing hard, I inadvertently inhale a deep whiff and start dry heaving uncontrollably.

"Jesus, Paul," I choke. "What died inside of you?"

Ignoring my comment, Paul finishes wiping and tosses a long line of soiled toilet paper out from behind. He clearly doesn't factor in the power or direction of the wind, as an updraft catches the waste, blowing it over him, across Frank's lap and onto Frank's oar, where it becomes entangled.

Frank says nothing. A sheepish look crosses Paul's face.

"Sorry, lads," he says and slips back below deck.

I read somewhere that the relationship between teammates on a polar expedition is similar to that of inmates in prison, with suspicion, resentment, and anger ruling their world.

Fortunately, we've been free from most of that. We're all still on excellent terms but, nonetheless, we're all eager to get the job done.

It's not long before a cabin appears along the shoreline and then another. Soon we're seeing cabins every few minutes. We're getting close; we all can sense it. Paul and Denis take a break from their rowing, turning to one another and taking out their pipes. The end is literally in sight. I open the hatch door and clamber out on deck.

"How'd it go?" I ask.

Denis has his fleece pulled up tight and a wool hat on. I see how slim he's become.

"It all feels surreal," he says. "We'll be home in a few days. It seemed so far away at the start..." He shakes his head as his voice trails off, and he pulls on his pipe.

All the dreams, all the anxiety, all the planning to get this expedition off the ground and now we're done. Paul and Denis are fantasizing about good food and drink back home; they've been talking about it for days and are talking about it now. Frank is quiet in his thoughts and leans against the spare oars that form our deck railing, but I know he's focused on finishing. I am too; I miss my girls terribly.

But it's easy to get lost in wanting the experience to end and miss being in the experience *now*. I always try to catch myself doing this when I'm on an expedition, and I've had to do a lot of catching on this journey. All too often, we live in our memories or our aspirations while neglecting the life we're living as we're living it.

"Let's enjoy the moment, guys," I say. "We'll never see this again."

VIDEO DIARY, DAY 55

DENIS: We have one more shift to go. Just pulled into the wet sleeping bag for the last time.

PAUL: We've worked our bollocks off for the past two months. It's pretty cool to see our little boat coming into Cambridge Bay. The two old lads are on the oars now. It's all a bit surreal now.

DENIS: First things first: we gotta get ourselves into the shower. We're all pretty filthy. I mean, joking aside, after fifty-four days plus the road trip up, we had one shower in between, there hasn't been a lot else going on, so the reality is that the shower is going to be fucking fantastic.

PAUL: It's mad how you really appreciate the really basic things, though. I hope it doesn't wear off completely.

DENIS: I'm not sure what to think at the moment.

IT'S THE AFTERNOON of August 28, 2013. Seeking out more protected waters, we pass to the north of a small island at the mouth of the inlet that leads to Cambridge Bay. We row inland, stopping a few times to film and photograph. An airplane rises from behind a small hill and we see antennae and satellite dishes just beyond. At the end of the inlet sits the village of Cambridge Bay, a dense grouping of low buildings in an otherwise uninterrupted rocky landscape. A group of boats cluster around a lone metal-faced dock. We pull into an open spot on the far side and Denis clambers up a ladder to the top. Paul tosses him the bowline. "Yaaahoooo!" he bellows with a hearty laugh. "Cambridge Bay, baby! We're done!"

And that's how it ends: no fanfare, no cameras, no people waiting or waving, just the four of us exhilarated and exhausted knowing our quest has come to a conclusion. We shake hands, hug, take photos, and strip out of our gear.

"We need to find a washing machine and a shower... and quick," Denis says, laughing.

We stumble about town in a daze. We find a place to stay, arrange flights, talk with locals, and connect with family.

"It'll take a few weeks before it all really sinks in," Paul says, knowing full well we'll need some psychological distance to see this tumultuous journey in its entirety. For now, we're just happy it's over.

On several occasions through the expedition, Arianna, my youngest daughter, asked, "Daddy, are you going to be home for my birthday?" Her birthday is September 17. We fly out of Cambridge Bay on August 29 and land in Vancouver the day after that.

On Friday, September 3, less than a week after our arrival in Cambridge Bay, the Canadian Coast Guard rescues the *Dangerous Waters* jet skiers on Franklin Strait just north of King William Island. Expedition leader Steve Moll explains what happened.

"We wake up in the morning and we're locked in the ice. The ice has moved in, it's completely around all the jet skis and the boat."[1] Moll is forced to call for rescue. "Everyone has a point where you're going to break, and Mother Nature here in the Arctic can break you like nothing else I've ever seen."[2]

Hearing about the rescue of Moll and his team reinforces the certainty that our decision to stop in Cambridge Bay was the correct one. If motorized craft needed rescue, then a human-powered craft had no chance at all. We traveled for 54 days and covered a distance of 1,163 miles. We didn't make it to Pond Inlet as we'd hoped, but we were afforded many opportunities to speak with people who live in the Arctic and experience their land in a way few others have. The climate change deniers that have followed our journey label us idiots and failures, but it doesn't bother me now as it did before. The scientific consensus about human-caused climate change and its likely effects is so overwhelming that these voices are nothing but hecklers in an otherwise rational discourse. The media as a whole is supportive of our expedition and paints a fair picture of our effort. CBS runs a feature story about the trip on their Saturday-night evening news, staunchly defending our assertions that climate change is real and that the Arctic is changing. Our journey, with all its hair-raising challenges, has successfully captured attention, and it appears people are hearing our message.

This year proved to be cold by recent standards, but even so, the minimum ice extent is the sixth-lowest ever recorded—a staggering 0.55 million square miles below the 1981–2010 average, equivalent to the area of British Columbia and Yukon combined.

The Vancouver Aquarium's Director of Arctic Programs Eric Solomon put it in perspective for me shortly after the completion of our journey: "The ice that you guys encountered says more about where the ice was over the last two months than how much ice there has been overall. There is, for example, a big hole in the ice near the North Pole right now. Meanwhile, the winds have been blowing a lot of ice down into the archipelago and into the region where you guys have been rowing. As long as there's any ice at all, it will blow around. In fact, we can expect to see more winds blowing from different directions than they used to as the climate changes." Solomon's words echo what the Elders told us and what we intuitively understood. "Many factors affect how much ice there is, where it is, and how thick it is in any one place in the massive Arctic. The weather in the Arctic can be unpredictable and is getting more so. The mistake we sometimes make is thinking weather can tell us something about the climate. Weather happens locally over a short period of time. Sometimes it's cold; sometimes it's warm; sometimes it's raining; sometimes it's not. You guys experienced weather. Climate is something we measure over decades. This summer's Arctic weather barely even impacted that long-term trend line at all."

Every person we spoke to on our voyage made it clear that climate change is affecting the Arctic. They had no ulterior motives or hidden agendas; they simply shared their experiences. For me, their voices hold a value few others do, yet for some reason they go unheard. And it's been that way for centuries.

Just a couple of hundred miles from our finishing point in Cambridge Bay, Parks Canada had been searching for Franklin's lost ships *Erebus* and *Terror*. When I walked the beaches of King William Island with Louie Kamookak in 2007, he told me he was searching for the ships in his small sixteen-foot aluminum motorboat.

"How can you possibly search an area that is over a thousand square kilometers in such a small boat?" I asked, perplexed.

"There's an island out there that my people call Umiaktalik. It means 'the place of the boat.' It's where I look."

"You mean, no one's looked there yet?" I asked in disbelief. "You'd think it'd be the first place they'd look." But I was wrong.

Much of Inuit oral history had been dismissed over the years as inaccurate or untrue.[3] Louie explained that Inuit history indicates that a ship sank in shallow water, its masts remaining visible for two seasons before they disappeared. The evidence has been there all along but remained ignored, until just recently. On September 2, 2014, Parks Canada discovered the wreck of the *Erebus* near the island of Umiaktalik, lying perfectly upright in only thirty-six feet of water. Its masts would have protruded above the sea when it sat on the seabed. Inuit oral history was right.

The people of the North—the same people we ignored when they told us where to look for Franklin's lost ships—now tell us the Arctic is changing. They speak of strange and inconsistent weather patterns becoming the new normal, of their homes sinking into the melting permafrost, of different animals appearing in their waters and on their land, of a shorter winter season and thinner ice, of an entire ecosystem in upheaval before their eyes.

And those voices aren't alone; they're supported by Western science. The Intergovernmental Panel on Climate Change has spelled it out in each report it's produced since its inception in 1988. Every national academy of science in the world is raising the alarm, as are the World Bank and the International Energy Agency. Ninety-seven percent of all climate scientists are screaming at us to take heed. The message is clear: global warming is happening, and it's posing a clear and present danger to our civilization.

The climate crisis had its birth in the late 1700s as the Industrial Revolution ushered in an era of unprecedented prosperity and growth, and with it the misguided notion that humankind can dominate and control the natural world. Our population numbers exploded (during the twentieth century alone, it swelled from 1.6 billion to 6.1 billion people), as did our ecological footprint, and fossil fuels quickly became the lifeblood of the industrial machine. It's taken only two centuries of emissions to bring us to the brink of irreversible catastrophe.

But how do we tackle the climate crisis when doing so will require that we dismantle the socioeconomic machine that brought us here? Our entire political and social order is linked to a growth-based, profit-seeking economic system that panics at the thought of anything hindering GDP growth.

I firmly believe humankind can make the changes necessary to avoid a climate disaster, but we're going to need a powerful stimulus to do so, and I fear that by the time we have that stimulus, it will be too late. As it stands, we need to make immediate and massive transformations to have any hope of limiting warming to 2 degrees Celsius. The International Energy Agency warns that we need to get emissions under control by 2017 to avoid becoming "locked in" to critically dangerous warming, because once carbon is emitted into the atmosphere, it stays there for hundreds of years. As the IEA's chief economist, Fatih Birol, sees it, "The door to reach two degrees is about to close. In 2017 it will be closed forever."[4]

In 2011, a London-based think tank called the Carbon Tracker Initiative undertook a groundbreaking study that tallied up all the coal, gas, and oil reserves as claimed by fossil fuel companies, private and state-owned, worldwide. It showed that the fossil fuels already on the books of these companies and making profits for shareholders—the fuels that must be burned for these companies to stay solvent—will generate 2,795 gigatons of carbon dioxide when burned. Climate scientists estimate that, if we are to have any hope of staying below a 2-degree-Celsius increase in temperatures, we cannot dump more than 565 gigatons of carbon into the atmosphere by midcentury.[5] The conundrum is clear. In the words of American environmentalist Bill McKibben, "The thing to notice is, 2,795 is five times 565. It's not even close." It's a life-and-death contest between the fossil fuel industry and the planet. The fossil fuel industry has every intention of burning five times more fossil fuel than the Earth's atmosphere can safely absorb.[6] And if they do, we'll all lose.

Humankind has enacted sweeping changes many times in the past, during wartime, pandemics, and after natural disasters. But the changes we're being asked to make now are different. They're proactive rather than reactive. They will try to prevent something from happening in the future rather than reacting to something that's already happened. It's difficult to digest, and even more difficult to act upon, but if we do nothing—if we simply continue doing exactly what we've been doing all along—we will be guaranteed chaos and disaster. The zeitgeist of our time—driven by our free-market economy, which necessitates constant, unending growth and development as if it were the only road forward—must change before we can have a hope of addressing climate change.

The Gaia theory, postulated by chemist James Lovelock in the 1970s, states that organisms interact with their inorganic surroundings on Earth to form a complex, self-regulating system that maintains conditions for life on the planet. If something upsets the planetary balance, the Earth itself will shift in some way and find stability. Humankind, in its unquenchable desire to grow and expand, is upsetting the planetary balance and with that come consequences. Climate change is one of the biggest consequences to date, and with it is coming an existential crisis for our species.

ILIRA. AS THE specter of climate change looms over the world, we should all be feeling it. There's no doubt we have the intelligence to understand what is happening and the reasoning to figure out what has to be done; the only question is whether we have the courage to see things through.

Ilira can overwhelm and incapacitate as much as it can energize and inspire. From that first storm on the Beaufort Sea to our encounters with belugas, bowheads, and bears, from the many long forced waits we've endured while winds howled around us to our close call with several tons of pack ice, from our ongoing astonishment at the size of the seas here in the North to our delight in the nightly light shows as we closed in on the end of the trip, *ilira* has been our constant companion on this journey. Our fear could easily have paralyzed us on many occasions, but instead it forced us into action—whatever drastic, dramatic, and often improvised action was necessary for us to survive and to leave us in awe of what we'd lived through, and of life itself.

In the Arctic, where life often turns on a decision made in a moment, *ilira* is present every day. To people who live in the North, the impacts of climate change on daily life and the need for dramatic action are readily apparent. For people who live to the south, where the ecosystem is much less fragile and life is much easier, it's more difficult to think about a place that's so far away it seems surreal, as if what's happening there has no relevance to daily life on the rest of the planet, much less as if what's happening there could be a harbinger of things to come for all of humanity.

But if humanity is going to survive climate change, we're going to have to get past the idea that what's happening in the Arctic is distant, surreal, and irrelevant to the rest of us. What's happening in the Far North is not only a harbinger of things to come but an indicator of things that are already happening. The signs and symptoms of climate change are all around us, all the time. Extreme weather events are more common now, there are stronger and more frequent hurricanes, coral reefs are dying, glaciers are receding, the ice sheets of Greenland and Antarctica are disintegrating, the ocean is rising...

Climate change is here. It's already happening.

How we deal with it is up to us.

EPILOGUE

IT'S BEEN THREE YEARS NOW since our expedition across the
Arctic and, in that time, the need to do something about climate change has grown exponentially. Temperature data from
2014 revealed that it was the hottest year since record-taking
began in 1880, until that record was beaten in 2015. As I write
this in November 2016, NASA is predicting that this will sur-
pass 2015 and be the new hottest year on record. That's three
years in a row. The trend is terrifying.

Toward the end of 2015, we made a promising step forward in combating climate change with the adoption of the
Paris Agreement. In this climate accord, 195 countries from
the global community adopted the first-ever universal legally
binding climate deal that would limit global warming to below
2 degrees Celsius, with every effort to keep it to 1.5 degrees
Celsius. It came into force on November 4, 2016.

At first glance, the wording of the Paris Agreement is promising. It lays out meaningful targets and sets plans in place to avert climate disaster. But those in the know remain worried. Many experts and scientists have pointed out that the pledges made in the agreement are simply not enough to achieve the targets the agreement sets out. Distinguished climate scientist James Hansen, who has been at the forefront of climate issues for the last three decades, is very clear on this point: "It's just worthless words. There is no action, just promises. As long as fossil fuels appear to be the cheapest fuels out there, they will continue to be burned." The former NASA scientist, who has been accredited with bringing awareness of climate change to the world, understands all too well what needs to be done to avert disaster, and he's steaming mad. "It's a fraud really, a fake . . . It's just bullshit for them to say: 'We'll have a 2C warming target and then try to do a little better every five years.' "[1]

And it's not just Hansen raising the alarm. In its November 3, 2016, *Emissions Gap Report,* the United Nations Environment Programme (UNEP) said that the emission-cutting promises put forward in the Paris Agreement will allow temperatures to rise from 2.9 degrees Celsius to 3.4 degrees Celsius above preindustrial levels this century, well above the 2-degree ceiling that scientists consider the safety limit.[2] As for the 1.5-degree cap the Paris Agreement hopes we can achieve, few scientists consider that a realistic possibility, as the radical changes required to achieve such a target would be so profound that few politicians hoping to stay in power would ever seriously entertain enacting any legislation with enough punch to make that happen.

And that's just the politicians who are onside, not those who continue to openly question the reality of climate change and the fact that human activity is causing it. Even before the votes had been cast in the 2016 U.S. presidential election, the entire cast of candidates running for the Republican Party leadership had openly derided the science of climate change. And the winner, President Donald Trump, has gone so far as to say that climate change is just a hoax invented by the Chinese. Such oddball banter would be amusing if it weren't coming from arguably the most politically powerful man on earth, and leader of the most powerful nation on earth. How can we be expected to take the drastic and costly measures required to meet the Paris targets when conspicuously ill-informed voices like Trump's continue spreading doubt among a populace that is clearly misinformed enough to believe him?

But those are the changes we need to make to avert disaster; 97 percent of the climate science community tell us so. If 97 percent of doctors said that smoking caused cancer while a handful of politicians with backing from the tobacco industry decried them as wrong, who would you listen to?

If we don't take immediate action, we are knowingly headed for an avoidable human tragedy. We will be faced with a world ravaged by drought, hunger, and disease, where sea levels will rise over sixteen feet in just a few centuries, and where countless millions will be forced to escape an affliction of our own making, launching mass migrations that will dwarf the current and ongoing exodus from Syria. Climate change is not someone else's problem. It will affect us all.

As this book was entering the production process, I embarked on another journey to the Arctic, this time with my family. I wanted my wife and daughters to experience adventure and understand what makes their husband and father tick. But more than that, I wanted them to appreciate the Arctic the way I now appreciate it, and understand the urgency the way I now understand it.

Over the course of thirty-five days, my wife Nicky and I, along with our two daughters, Arianna and Caitlin (ten and twelve years old at the time), kayaked the length of Canada's longest river, the Mackenzie, 1,087 miles from Great Slave Lake to Inuvik, near the Arctic Ocean. The trip proved to be everything I hoped it would be and more. It opened the eyes of my loved ones to a world they'd only heard about from me and allowed them to see firsthand the majesty that is our North. Few Canadians have an opportunity to see and experience a landscape that encompasses approximately 40 percent of our country. I'm deeply gratified to have been able to pass along my profound appreciation of the Arctic to those I care about most.

They have learned to appreciate, as I do, the uniqueness of a world that shuns night altogether for the months of its summer, and a wilderness so vast that all sense of mastery is hastily overwhelmed. They appreciate the lives of the people who call the Arctic home and thrive in a land where most of us would struggle to survive. They appreciate a remoteness so complete that even a footprint of our species seems lost, but without being so.

More than that, they appreciate that humanity's excesses are being felt in the Arctic even where humanity is nowhere to be seen. They experienced this firsthand on our journey, when we experienced unprecedented heat for weeks and were enveloped in thick suffocating smoke from the incessant fires that now ravage the Boreal forests of the North. They experienced it through the stories we heard of new animals and birds frequenting the region, and even saw for themselves a muskox where none had ever been seen before.

While in the North, we learned of lightning storms more frequent than ever before, of strange and unpredictable weather patterns, and of precipitation that no longer rains down from above but pours. As we drifted north of the Arctic Circle, we were dismayed to see the slumping banks of the Mackenzie River disintegrating as melting permafrost loosened their grip. As a family, we experienced the Arctic as a world beautiful and raw but also vulnerable to change, delicately balanced on the cusp of something none of us can quite predict.

The time capsule I hid for my girls on Sellwood Bay remains there, and after this trip I sense in them a greater desire to return one day and find it. I wonder what the Arctic will be like when they do. Will it be the place they remember from this trip, or will it by then be completely unrecognizable, transformed by a world out of control?

As I said in the introduction, I wish I could take every reader of this book on a journey to the Arctic as I did my family, to instill that appreciation in so many more people. I can't, but I can hope this book acts as my surrogate and in helping you understand the magnitude of the problem we face. Do we keep moving forward as we have, knowingly jeopardizing the future of generations to come? Or do we find the foresight, selflessness, and humanity to take actions that may not bear fruit in our lifetimes but will undoubtedly chart a better course for our great-grandchildren and theirs?

The choice is ours.

NOTES

CHAPTER 1: A LAST FIRST

1   Alex Morales, "Kyoto Veterans Say Global Warm-
    ing Goal Slipping Away," *Bloomberg*, November 4, 2013,
    https://www.bloomberg.com/news/articles/2013-11-04/
    kyoto-veterans-say-global-warming-goal-slipping-away.

2   World Bank, "Climate Change Report Warns of Dramatically Warmer
    World This Century," press release, November 18, 2012,
    http://www.worldbank.org/en/news/feature/2012/11/18/Climate-
    change-report-warns-dramatically-warmer-world-this-century.

CHAPTER 2: IT BEGINS

1   Katia Moskvitch, "Mysterious Siberian Crater Attributed to
    Methane," *Nature,* July 31, 2014, http://www.nature.com/news/
    mysterious-siberian-crater-attributed-to-methane-1.15649.

2   Terrence McCoy, "Scientists May Have Cracked the
    Giant Siberian Crater Mystery—and the News Isn't
    Good," *Washington Post,* August 5, 2014, https://www.
    washingtonpost.com/news/morning-mix/wp/2014/08/05/

scientists-may-have-cracked-the-giant-siberian-crater-mystery-and-
the-news-isnt-good/.

3   Alyssa Navarro, "Thawing of Permafrost in Alaska Could
Begin by 2070: How This Could Accelerate Global Warming,"
Tech Times, October 24, 2015, http://www.techtimes.com/
articles/98766/20151024/thawing-of-permafrost-in-alaska-
could-begin-by-2070-how-this-could-accelerate-global-warming.
htm#sthash.mblZejQy.dpuf.

4   "Climate Change Could Cause Alaskan Permafrost to Melt and
Release Methane into the Atmosphere," Americans.org (n.d.),
http://americans.org/climate-change-could-cause-alaskan-
permafrost-to-melt-and-release-methane-into-the-atmosphere.

5   At 340 and 370 tons, respectively, Franklin's ships, *Erebus* and
Terror, were behemoths compared to the 47-ton *Gjøa*. The water of
King William Island's eastern channel was very shallow and even
Amundsen's tiny *Gjøa* ran aground on a rocky reef, nearly scuttling
the boat and forcing the crew to toss gear and provisions overboard in
a desperate attempt to free it. There's little doubt that Franklin's much
larger ships would have become hopelessly grounded, but no one
will ever know for sure.

6   Roald Amundsen, *Roald Amundsen: My Life as an Explorer*
(Garden City, NY: Doubleday, Page, 1927).

7   Mike de Souza, "Stephen Harper's Environment Minister Casts Doubt
on Climate Change," Canada.com, October 3, 2013, http://o.canada.
com/news/stephen-harpers-environment-minister-casts-doubt-on-
climate-change.

CHAPTER 4: TUKTOYAKTUK

1   Naomi Klein, *This Changes Everything: Capitalism vs. the
Climate* (Toronto: Knopf, 2014), 36.

2   Environics Institute, "Focus Canada 2013: Canadian Public
Opinion about Climate Change," November 18, 2013,
http://www.environicsinstitute.org.

3   Dan Kahan, "Fixing the Communications Failure," *Nature* 463
(January 2010): 296-97, doi:10.1038/463296ab.

4   L.A. Harwood, P. Norton, B. Day, and P. Hall, "The Harvest of Beluga Whales in Canada's Western Arctic: Hunter-Based Monitoring of the Size and Composition of the Catch," Canadian Stock Assessment Secretariat Research Document 2000/141 (Ottawa: Fisheries and Oceans, 2000), http://www.dfo-mpo.gc.ca/CSAS/Csas/DocREC/2000/PDF/2000_141e.pdf.

5   Cynthia T. Tynan and Douglas P. DeMaster, "Observations and Predictions of Arctic Climate Change: Potential Effects on Marine Mammals," *Arctic* 50, (December 1997): 315, doi:10.14430/arctic1113.

CHAPTER 5: DRAGGING ON THE TUKTOYAKTUK PENINSULA

1   Philip Torrens, "Predatory Rites" (n.d.), http://www.summitstudios.biz/spotlight_torrens_sample.asp.

CHAPTER 6: NEAR DISASTER ON FRANKLIN BAY

1   Northwest Territories, Environment and Natural Resources, "Barren-Ground Caribou: Northern Herds" (n.d.), http://www.enr.gov.nt.ca/node/2979.

2   CBC News, "N.W.T. Caribou Populations Continue to Decline, Survey Shows," September 28, 2015, http://www.cbc.ca/news/canada/north/bluenose-east-bathurst-caribou-herds-continue-to-decline-1.3247057.

CHAPTER 7: MESSAGE IN A BOTTLE

1   John Walsh, Donald Wuebbles, et al., "Melting Ice," in *Climate Change Impacts in the United States: The Third National Climate Assessment,* ed. J.M. Mellilo, Terese Richmond, and G.W. Yohe (U.S. Global Change Research Program, 2014), http://nca2014.globalchange.gov/report/our-changing-climate/melting-ice.

2   Emily J. Gertz, "Here's Why the Northeast's Next Winter Is Going to Be Freakishly Cold," *TakePart*, August 31, 2015, http://www.takepart.com/article/2015/08/31/arctic-sea-ice-melt-global-warming-extreme-cold-winters/.

3   Ibid.

CHAPTER 9: THE BEACHES OF THE DOLPHIN AND UNION STRAIT

1 Ocean Portal Team, "Ocean Acidification," Smithsonian National Museum of Natural History, 2016, http://ocean.si.edu/ocean-acidification.

2 Jillian Kestler-D'Amours, "NASA Pinpoints Rise in Sea Levels," *Toronto Star,* August 28, 2015, https://www.thestar.com/news/world/2015/08/28/nasa-pinpoints-rise-in-sea-levels.html.

3 Helen Briggs, "US Sea Level North of New York City 'Jumped by 128mm,'" *BBC News*, February 24, 2015, http://www.bbc.com/news/science-environment-31604953.

4 Mark Hertsgaard, "Climate Seer James Hansen Issues His Direst Forecast Yet," *The Daily Beast,* July 20, 2015, http://www.thedailybeast.com/articles/2015/07/20/climate-seer-james-hansen-issues-his-direst-forecast-yet.html.

5 Hertsgaard, "Climate Seer James Hansen."

6 Chris D'Angelo, "Rapidly Melting Glacier Will Raise Sea Levels 'for Decades to Come,'" *Huffington Post,* November 12, 2015, http://www.huffingtonpost.com/entry/melting-greenland-glacier-rising-sea-levels_us_56451775e4b08cda34883038.

7 Nicholas Stern, *The Economics of Climate Change: The Stern Review* (Cambridge: Cambridge University Press, 2007).

8 Klein, *This Changes Everything,* 13.

9 NASA, "Heat Intensifies Siberian Wildfires," NASA Earth Observatory, August 2, 2013, http://earthobservatory.nasa.gov/IOTD/view.php?id=81736.

10 Brian Kahn, "Northern Canada Is on Fire, and It's Making Global Warming Worse," *Mother Jones,* July 18, 2014, http://www.motherjones.com/environment/2014/07/canada-wildfires-climate-change-feedbacks.

11 Marc Montgomery, "NWT: Worst Forest Fire Season in Decades," RCI *Radio Canada International*, July 15, 2014, http://www.rcinet.ca/en/2014/07/15/worst-forest-fire-season-in-decades/.

12 Maureen Langlois, "Tundra Fires and Climate Change: More Bad News," *The Two-Way* (NPR), July 28, 2011, http://www.npr.org/sections/thetwo-way/2011/07/28/138789103/tundra-fires-and-climate-change-more-bad-news.

CHAPTER 10: ESCAPE TO VICTORIA ISLAND

1   Ed Struzik, "Grizzly Bears on Ice," *National Wildlife* (National
    Wildlife Federation), February 1, 2006, http://www.nwf.org/
    news-and-magazines/national-wildlife/animals/archives/2006/
    grizzly-bears-on-ice.aspx.

2   A 2014 University of California–Berkeley study suggests that
    the split may be as recent as 500,000 years ago; Hannah Hoag,
    "Polar Bears Diverged from Brown Bears Fairly Recently," *Nature,*
    May 10, 2014, https://www.scientificamerican.com/article/
    polar-bears-diverged-from-brown-bears-fairly-recently/.

3   Polar Bears International, "Climate Change" (n.d.), http://www.
    polarbearsinternational.org/about-polar-bears/climate-change.

4   Struzik, "Grizzly Bears on Ice."

5   Matt McGrath, "Polar Bears Fail to Adapt to Lack of Food in Warmer
    Arctic," *BBC News*, July 16, 2015, http://www.bbc.com/news/
    science-environment-33551569.

6   Lisa Johnson, "Ian Stirling, Polar Bear Scientist, Wins
    $50K Lifetime Achievement Award," *CBC News*, December 9,
    2015, http://www.cbc.ca/news/canada/british-columbia/
    ian-stirling-polar-bear-weston-foundation-1.3357587.

7   Henry Duff Traill, *The Life of Sir John Franklin, R.N.*
    (New York: J. Murray, 1896), 217.

CHAPTER 11: *ILIRA*

1   Tristin Hopper, "Reality TV Stars Crossing Northwest Passage on
    Jet Skis Forced to Cancel Arctic Trek after Costly Rescue," *National
    Post,* September 13, 2013, http://news.nationalpost.com/news/
    canada/crew-filming-reality-tv-show-forced-to-cancel-trek-through-
    northwest-passage-on-jet-skis-after-costly-rescue.

2   CBC News, "Reality TV Jet Skiers Rescued in Northwest Passage,"
    September 6, 2013, http://www.cbc.ca/news/canada/north/
    reality-tv-jet-skiers-rescued-in-northwest-passage-1.1699868.

3   After our trek on the shores of King William Island, CBC's Evan
    Solomon made a documentary of our expedition that aired on the CBC
    national Sunday-night news. The documentary, called "Death in the
    Arctic," questioned indifference to solving the Franklin mystery and

may have ruffled some feathers. The following year Parks Canada announced funding to search for the lost ships. Thanks to the work of Louie Kamookak, the wreckage of HMS *Erebus* was found on September 2, 2014, by a Parks Canada team led by Ryan Harris and Marc-André Bernier. On September 12, 2016, it was announced that the wreck of HMS *Terror* had been found submerged in Terror Bay, off the southwest coast of King William Island.

4   Klein, *This Changes Everything,* 25.

5   Alan Rusbridger, "Climate Change: Why *The Guardian* Is Putting Threat to Earth Front and Centre," *The Guardian,* March 6, 2015, https://www.theguardian.com/environment/2015/mar/06/climate-change-guardian-threat-to-earth-alan-rusbridger.

6   Bill McKibben, "The Thing to Notice," speech, Do the Math tour, 350.org, New York City, November 16, 2012.

EPILOGUE

1   Oliver Milman, "James Hansen, Father of Climate Change Awareness, Calls Paris Talks 'a Fraud,'" *The Guardian,* December 12, 2015, https://www.theguardian.com/environment/2015/dec/12/james-hansen-climate-change-paris-talks-fraud.

2   United Nations Environment Programme (UNEP), *The Emissions Gap Report 2016: A UNEP Synthesis Report* (Nairobi: UNEP, 2016), http://uneplive.unep.org/media/docs/theme/13/EGR_2015_Technical_Report_final_version.pdf.